OPEN FOR BUSINESS

OPEN FOR BUSINESS

THE INSIDER'S GUIDE TO
LEASING COMMERCIAL REAL ESTATE

TYLER CAUBLE

LIONCREST
PUBLISHING

OPEN FOR BUSINESS
The Insider's Guide to Leasing Commercial Real Estate

ISBN   978-1-61961-723-0 *Paperback*
      978-1-61961-724-7 *Ebook*

For my grandfather, Roy, who taught me the value of work ethic, but more importantly, what it means to be a man.

CONTENTS

INTRODUCTION 9

PART ONE: FIND YOUR SPACE

1. DETERMINE YOUR NEEDS 25

2. ASSEMBLE YOUR A-TEAM 47

3. COMPARE POTENTIAL SPACES 71

PART TWO: NEGOTIATING THE LEASE

4. GIVE-AND-TAKE..91

5. SIGN THE LEASE...105

6. BUILD-OUTS 119

CONCLUSION 135

GLOSSARY 141

ABOUT THE AUTHOR 159

INTRODUCTION

LEASING COMMERCIAL REAL ESTATE

Denise is a massage therapist who's been working from her home and the homes of her clients. Her business is growing, and she's looking for a space to open a studio, hopefully in a neighborhood that is near medical offices. She's never rented a commercial space but thinks it's the right thing to do to take her business to the next level. She's worried about a landlord taking advantage of her lack of experience and has no idea where to start looking or what to do next.

Sound familiar? Small businesses often start like Denise's, out of a basement or without a space of their own. As the business grows, so does the need to expand. Did you know that choosing the right location is one of the top five contributors to the success of a business? It's an important decision, and you need to get it right.

Luckily, you don't have to figure it out on your own. This book will take you through the steps of determining your space requirements, choosing the appropriate space, and negotiating the lease. It will also introduce you to the professionals who can help you do these things more effectively and efficiently—saving you money and headaches in the long run.

THE COMPLEXITY OF COMMERCIAL REAL ESTATE

This book is for any small business owner who needs commercial space. Perhaps you're tired of working out of your garage or want to open a brand-new business that requires a storefront. You may need space for a second or third location for your already thriving business. Regardless of the reason, the space you choose is vital to your bottom line.

The process of leasing commercial real estate is complicated, because every lease is different, no property is alike, and the requirements of every business owner vary depending on the type of business they own. For example, professional offices have vastly different needs from retail spaces. A professional office might benefit from being on the top floor of a building, but retail would perish if not on the ground floor, where there's plenty of foot traffic and visibility.

The amount of space you need and how you will use the property are important considerations as well. Although there are some guidelines, there's no minimum square footage required. You can find cubicles in coworking spaces or Amazon-like manufacturing spaces and warehouses. Some spaces are acceptable as-is, and others will require some tender love and care to get them ready. Restaurants might need to keep waiting areas and industry-specific regulations in mind.

Even if you already have an idea of the type and size of space you need, there are other considerations. Before you get started, you need to answer questions such as the following: How do you go about finding a site? Where do you even start looking? Is the lease negotiable? Who will pay for the new carpet and paint, if necessary? Do you need an attorney? And that's just scratching the surface.

Commercial real estate is complex, and you are at a distinct disadvantage if you don't understand the process. Unlike the apartment lease you didn't read and still signed in college, a commercial lease is a unique and multifaceted document. Like everything else in your business, it pays to understand the specifics. It's just good sense to know what you are agreeing to—you will be legally responsible for *every single word* in the contract, whether you understand it or not.

WHAT A BUSINESS OWNER NEEDS TO KNOW

It seems a little unfair to require you to become an expert in the leasing process just as your business is expanding and requiring more time and attention. Yet, making wrong decisions in a long-term lease can have devastating consequences for your business.

Entering into a commercial lease is a business transaction. You'll be negotiating with a landlord who is an expert. He may have multiple properties and has perfected his lease with a team of other professionals who help him manage his business. Although you need to understand the steps that you'll go through on your way to a new workspace, there are professionals who can help you, too. You don't have to do it alone—nor should you.

A commercial real estate broker can protect your interests from start to finish. Commercial brokers specialize in finding the best properties, negotiating leases, and helping you circumnavigate the entire leasing process. They take the stress out of leasing a new space and can guide you through the process so you meet the landlord on equal ground. In fact, negotiating without your own broker is like going into a gunfight with a stick: you're not going to win.

It's tempting to do your own negotiating. After all, you know your business, you've negotiated deals before, and this is just a lease. Unfortunately, it's not that easy, and a commercial lease is never "just a lease." Commercial leases are complicated legal documents, and every point can be negotiated when you know what to ask for.

Consider John, the successful owner of a hip music store who decided to open a bar in a not-so-hip part of town. He had no idea there were commercial brokers who could help him, so he negotiated his own lease with the landlord and opened his doors. Over time, the neighborhood changed, and the bar started to gain traction. His business made the entire neighborhood a destination, other businesses moved into the area, and the not-so-hip part of town became the place everyone wanted to be.

The landlord watched this metamorphosis and saw a chance to profit. He decided he would not renew John's lease and instead open up his own bar in the building, using John's equipment and customer base. Sadly, there's not a happy ending to this story. John had no choice but to close his doors. He was put out of business essentially because he wasn't protected under his lease. He didn't know that he could have negotiated options in the very beginning that would have allowed him to stay for an extended period of time. He didn't know that he should have gotten help before agreeing to the deal.

Keep in mind that it's not just help that you need; it's the *right kind of help*. Although you may be tempted to call on your residential real estate agent, residential and commercial real estate are quite different. Not only is there no central listing source for commercial real estate, but the negotiation processes are like night and day, so you need someone knowledgeable in the commercial market and current listings.

Commercial documents also differ significantly. Unlike standardized residential forms, every commercial lease is different and will vary depending on the property and the landlord. John's cautionary tale proves the point that specific knowledge regarding the negotiation of commercial leases may decide the future fate of your business.

THE PROCESS

Each chapter in this book describes a step or two in the process of finding and leasing a space. We'll cover them in depth, but an overview will be helpful as a road map, so you know where we're going.

STEP 1: RUN YOUR NUMBERS

Before you start to look for a property, you have to figure out your costs. Talk to your business and financial advisers and determine what you can afford. If you have a broker at this point, bring them into the discussion.

If you're moving out of your garage or home office, you're going from zero overhead to what may be thousands of dollars in rent. Be realistic and make sure your business can weather the change.

STEP 2: DEFINE YOUR NEEDS

Determining exactly what you require in a property will make the search more efficient. Think about where you need to be and any specific features you must have. For example, do you need to be near the interstate? Perhaps your clients are within a certain neighborhood and being near major highways isn't important. Or perhaps you're a service company and easy highway access is crucial. You don't want your service people driving all day to get back and forth to the office after service calls.

Knowing your specific site requirements up front will save time and energy. Do you need to be in the business district? Do you need to be surrounded by other, complementary businesses? Are you willing to pay more rent to be in a popular location?

The physical space is also an important consideration. The space you choose may need to be modified. For example, you might need cubicles, meeting rooms, or a specific amount of storage space. The more thorough you can be regarding your needs, the more apt you are to find the perfect space (and not settle for second best).

STEP 3: ASSEMBLE YOUR A-TEAM

Once you have an idea of what you want, it's time to start bringing in the right team to help you. Your team might include a commercial real estate broker, an attorney, or a business coach. If you start with a broker, he can help you find the other professionals needed to get the task accomplished. Experienced brokers can make good recommendations for everything from accountants to zoning.

STEP 4: FOCUS ON YOUR BUSINESS

Don't neglect your business during the real estate search. You've assembled an expert team to help, so now it's time to relax and let them do their job. Communicate with your broker, but let them do the leg work. It can take time to find the perfect space. Focus on your business as it continues to grow, and you'll be ready for the move when the time comes.

STEP 5: TOUR YOUR SITES

Your broker will prequalify sites for you based on your requirements. He'll bring together as many properties as possible and then help you narrow the list. You will then tour the optimal sites, preferably on the same day so that you can make the best comparisons.

STEP 6: WEIGH YOUR OPTIONS

Finding the right space is an emotional journey, but you need to look at all of the possibilities as logically and analytically as possible. There's always room for "it just feels right," but you must also compare the properties based on all of the variables.

STEP 7: NEGOTIATE YOUR LEASE

As I've said before (and will continue to stress), every landlord will have a different lease, so it's critical to read and understand each clause. A good broker can review it with you. He knows what should and shouldn't be in the lease and can make recommendations. It's more cost-effective if your broker can make recommendations before sending the lease to your attorney for review.

STEP 8: OPEN FOR BUSINESS

After signing on the dotted line, you're ready to move in, unless a "build-out" is necessary. When the space isn't designed to suit your needs, a build-out is the work needed to get it ready. It can be anything from paint and carpet to moving the walls or adding a kitchen.

Once the build-out is complete, you're ready for business. Remember that you have a continuing responsibility to stay compliant with your lease. If you follow the terms of your lease, you'll avoid penalties and enjoy the extra elbowroom without issues. You never want to find yourself in default, as you could get evicted from your space.

YOUR SECRET WEAPON

Finding and leasing commercial real estate is much easier

when you understand the process. Although you can use a shotgun approach and drive through neighborhoods, look for signs, or use Craigslist, the better alternative is to work with a commercial broker. This is the sniper approach, focused and efficient. Landlords know what they're doing, and they still have a team of knowledgeable, experienced professionals on their side.

Commercial brokers are your secret weapon. They can save you time and energy by curating appropriate properties to meet your needs. They know where the properties are and will save you time by only showing you the contenders. They can save you money—and future pain—by negotiating the points in the lease with knowledge of what is possible and how to protect your interests. They can assist during your build-out if needed. Best of all, there's no cost to you. Allow your broker to do what they do best, and you can focus on what's most important— your growing business.

INVESTING IN COMMERCIAL REAL ESTATE

Commercial real estate can also be used as an investment strategy. As with leasing, there are several specific factors to consider to make sure your investment will be profitable. It's important to look the property over carefully, consider what it will be used for, and take the following factors into consideration.

- Location: Think about the type of business you will have on the property. Is the property close to suppliers? Is it convenient to get to for both customers and employees? Are there businesses close by that can provide for the needs of customers and employees, such as eateries? Is it close to residential centers or industrial centers, and how will this affect the type of business that is going to be run there? The importance of location as a contributor to the value of the property can't be overstressed.

- Size and condition: Again, the type of business you are planning to have on the property is important. Is there room on the property for the business to expand? Will you need parking, and is there enough space available for your needs? Is the property too big for the business you are planning? If the property is large, are you interested in housing more than one business there? Another consideration that goes hand in hand with size is the condition of the property. If the property has previously been home to a business that may have damaged the condition of the property, it may be difficult to make the property operational for certain uses.

Depending on the types of business you are trying to attract, this may detract from the value of the property.

- Type of business: Zoning laws may apply depending on the type of business you are looking to attract, and if these laws are quite stringent, it may decrease the value of the property. Make sure you look into city ordinances or regulations so there are no surprises.

As with leasing, it's important to have the right team of experts working for you. If purchasing commercial real estate is the right move for you or your business, make sure you give yourself the benefit of an experienced team to help with every aspect of finding and purchasing the perfect property to suit your needs.

PART ONE

FIND YOUR SPACE

1

DETERMINE YOUR NEEDS

The first steps toward your new and improved working space require an in-depth analysis of your costs and needs. It doesn't make sense to start looking at spaces until you know exactly what you're looking for and what you can afford. Start by consulting your business advisers, your CPA, your broker, and anyone else on your team to make sure you've thought of everything. Make a list of all your requirements and maybe add a wish or two.

FACING REALITY

Run the numbers to get a real picture of your situation. Does a new space make sense, or are you just tired of having employees working at your kitchen table? Perhaps you could outsource some of your tasks by sending your accounting and marketing to outside firms. Similarly, if you're tired of shipping product out of your garage, you may not necessarily need to expand. Instead of leasing a space and hiring people to pack and ship, talk to a product fulfillment center. With a little investigation and creativity, you may find ways to solve your problems without paying rent every month.

A commercial lease is a long-term business commitment. It's also a financial commitment that becomes a legal obligation once you sign that dotted line. You want to be completely certain that your business has grown enough to justify a move.

It can be scary to move into a space with monthly rent. Even if you think you can afford it right now, consider what might happen if you lost a major client or if your market changed. You're still on the hook for the payment and need to be prepared to make adjustments. If you can't afford at least $1,000 to $2,000 in rent, you may need to reconsider your options. Sometimes it just doesn't make financial sense to lease a space.

Depending on your business model, entering into a commercial lease may not make business sense either. Although having a separate space dedicated to your business may sound enticing, not everyone needs an office.

If you're an e-commerce business that outsources fulfillment or drop-ships, you can work from the coffee shop or your car. If you're a personal trainer, you can go to your clients instead of launching your business with a new gym. If you're just starting out and strapped for cash, don't commit to spending money for rent and overhead if you don't have to.

COWORKING SPACES: A NEW OPTION

The changing face of how we work has created new options for *where* we work. Coworking spaces are working environments that are shared by people not employed by the same organization. As more of the workforce seeks alternative employment as entrepreneurs, independent contractors, and telecommuters, coworking spaces have become more popular.

A coworking space can provide a flexible work environment as well as a connection to a diverse community. Even better, it gets you out of the garage or coffeehouse for a fraction of the cost of a long-term lease.

Typically, you can opt for a variety of services and only pay for what you need. There may be tiered memberships or even hourly rates if you need only a conference room once a month. For example, you might need three dedicated desks for yourself and two other employees, as well as receptionist services, office equipment, and a kitchen. Or you might require only a shared desk and a mailing address. Either way, you could find your solution in a shared work environment.

1. Size of your business and number of employees: More than ten employees may be too many to make coworking efficient or cost-effective.

2. Hours of operation: Are they fixed or flexible? Does your schedule match the schedule of the coworking environment?

3. Personality or vibe of the space

4. Cost: Can you afford it, and will it help you save money (as compared with a lease)?

5. Employee work habits: Will the collaborative atmosphere be embraced by your employees, or will it be too distracting?

6. Amenities: Are amenities such as internet, snacks, or a conference room included?

THE BEST REASONS FOR SEEKING A NEW SPACE

As a fledgling business or a business trying to scale, your finances will be more sound if you can keep your overhead low. Do more with less as long as you can to build a strong financial foundation. At some point, however, it will make sense to stop outsourcing and bring everything in-house—but it doesn't have to be *your* house!

You will know when the time has come to move to a bigger or better space. You may have more employees than the office can hold or have to meet clients in a neutral location so they don't see your workspace. In some businesses, a presence in the market is important, and you need to be somewhere people can find you. A sign and a professional office might bring you more traffic and help land more clients.

Storage is another good reason for leasing commercial space. It will be clear when you finally outgrow your garage. You'll know more space is a legitimate need when you have more product than you have room for, and there's nowhere to fulfill all the orders that are pouring in. Having that additional space will give you more room to scale as well, because you'll be able to buy product in larger quantities and pay less per item.

Need for a professional space can also be driven by a desire to improve your business identity. For some businesses, being on the top floor of a building conveys the clout needed to hook the best clients. After all, wouldn't you rather hire an attorney in the penthouse suite instead of in the strip mall next to the pawn shop?

Even if you have a functional space, it may not have the prestige that portrays the image you want. For example, consider the top-rated company that wanted to upgrade their client base and land the "big fish" everyone in the industry was courting. Their current space was nice enough, but it was in the suburbs, while the potential new clients were primarily in the city center. The company wondered if the prospects would be willing to drive twenty minutes just to meet with them.

The company was already successful, had proof of concept, and was very good at their job. Even so, they routinely lost clients to competitors who were in flashier offices in the downtown area, where they could wine and dine possible customers. The company looked for a bigger, better alternative, but ultimately decided to stay where they were. Even though they knew their image needed a boost, they didn't want to pay the freight for a downtown office. They also didn't land the "big fish."

The decision to move to a new or more expensive space must be weighed carefully. The company in the prior example erred on the side of caution and lost a potential client, but they were willing to trade that result for keeping their budget strong. There's no wrong decision when you carefully consider the possibilities.

You never want to lease a new space under the assumption that "if you build it, they will come." Sometimes a nicer space will pay for itself with more or higher-value clients, but don't count on it. However, if you can afford the new space with the clients you have, it's a calculated risk that won't land you on the wrong side of your rent payments.

FOUR CONSIDERATIONS TO DEFINE THE SPACE YOU NEED

Once you've confirmed that you have an immediate need for leasing commercial space, and you know you can afford it, there are four main areas of inquiry. To help you specifically define the type of space you need, consider the workspace, storage, location, and budget.

WORKSPACE

If you are changing spaces, you want to make sure the new space has the square footage that you need. A good range is 125 to 225 square feet per person, if you want to feel comfortable. It's a wide range but will give you a rough idea. This basically equates to a ten-by-twelve-foot office for one person. Additional spaces may be necessary as well. Dig deep to think about exactly what you want and need. Are common spaces a requirement? Waiting rooms? A kitchen or bathrooms?

Retail typically has more demands. The square footage required will depend heavily on what you're selling, but the ground floor is where you'll want to be. You've probably never heard someone say they won't visit a tech company because the offices are on the tenth floor, but can you imagine a clothing store anywhere but on street level? If your business is like a retail operation that has more of a revolving door and counts on walk-in customers, pay attention to this aspect of your workspace.

STORAGE

Another part of your workspace that deserves some consideration is the space that your clients *don't* see. Imagine walking into a high-end retail store with a well-designed shopping area. You walk in and immediately understand the brand and have the "wow" experience. You like being there and don't mind spending your money in such a beautiful venue.

Now imagine walking into the same beautiful space and having full view of the manager's office or the shipping-and-receiving area. Do you really want your customers seeing the stained coffee cups from the morning meeting, stray packing peanuts, or boxes of files that still need to be put away? Probably not. It's fine to want a big, open area, but you defeat your purpose if there's no place to store your vacuum cleaner. Think through these details before you finalize your plan.

LOCATION

It's widely understood that the most important charac-
teristic of real estate is its location. This maxim applies to
commercial real estate as well. Where you decide to base
your operation is a crucial consideration and completely
dependent on what your business needs.

Visibility can be important, but isn't always a necessity. Is
drive-by traffic important to you? If so, you may need to
be on the corner of a major thoroughfare. If not, you can
save money if your office can be tucked away out of sight.

If customers routinely come into your establishment,
accessibility must be addressed. Try to understand your
target market and make it easy for them not only to
find you but also to get to you physically. For example,
Starbucks knows that most of their traffic occurs in the
morning as people head to work. Starbucks intentionally
chooses to be on the "a.m. side" of the road. Similarly, if
you're a grocery store, you might be more interested in
the "p.m. side" of the road, because your customers are
going to pick up groceries on the way home from work.
Make it easy for your customers, and they will reward you
with their business. Your target market will always take
the path of least resistance.

Figuring out where you need to be is also very intuitive.

You know your business well, so you don't need to over-complicate things. Look at what your competitors are doing. Are they all in office buildings downtown? Maybe you should consider looking at office buildings downtown. On the other hand, if you're a chiropractor who wants to be on the ground floor, you probably don't want to be next to another chiropractor. Depending on your industry, locating adjacent to competitors can either benefit or hurt your business.

Keep an eye on the trends, which can also inform your decision. For example, many consumer service businesses have recently started moving into shopping centers. Mortgage companies, insurance agencies, and even family practitioners are finding value in being where people routinely shop. Although rent in these areas can be higher than in an office building, the businesses are seeing increases in revenue thanks to additional exposure from signage and the added convenience for their clientele.

Another trend is co-tenancy, or locating near complementary businesses. Have you ever noticed how all of the fast food chains or hotels are located at the very same exit off the interstate, or how all of the gas stations in town are near the same intersection? They know that customers are more likely to frequent an area with more options, and they all benefit from that.

If you look at shopping centers housing Target stores, you'll usually see the full range of complementary businesses. Knowing that Target draws a certain consumer—primarily moms—other businesses will piggyback on their clientele. It's one-stop shopping. You will often see female-oriented fitness centers, nail salons, or larger stores such as Kroger, Ulta Beauty, Kohl's, and World Market in the same shopping center. Depending on your industry or niche, this strategy can also work for you.

Parking is an aspect of location that can make or break your business. Typically, city codes will dictate parking requirements depending on usage. For example, a city might require "three per thousand," meaning three parking spaces per one thousand square feet of leasable space. This requirement will vary depending on the type of space you're leasing and the city you're in.

Restaurants require different parking regulations, perhaps up to ten per thousand, due to the higher volume of customers going in and out. Restaurants must pay attention to these requirements, as well as their own traffic. If your restaurant is too large for the parking capacity of the shopping center, you probably won't survive. Your customers will go across the street to a competitor who has plenty of parking or park in spaces assigned to other tenants. When the other tenants complain, you won't be allowed to use their parking spaces, and your capacity will fall.

Convenience is king. No one wants to struggle to find parking when it's easier to go somewhere else. Consider the restaurant located on a corner of one of the busiest streets in town. Amazing drive-by traffic seemed to guarantee their success. So why didn't it? The parking lot was around the back of the building and underground. Once you figured out where to park, you had to walk up a flight of stairs and down the block to get to the restaurant. Even a heavy-hitting national chain couldn't make a tough parking situation like that work.

While customers in major metropolitan areas might be accustomed to making a trek, this restaurant's customers were used to driving right up to the door. The business shriveled and died.

Pay attention to what your target expects. In big cities, you want to be as close as you can to public transportation, but a neighborhood bar in a smaller town should pay attention to the neighborhood's walkability. Know your audience and make visiting your business as stress-free as possible.

BUDGET

Know your budget and stick to it. Get advice from your accountant or CPA and understand all of the expenses associated with renting a new space. As discussed earlier, you have a better chance of success if you lease a new space knowing you can afford it even without additional sales. Although a high rent can be motivational, it can also be a death sentence.

Once you have a realistic budget in mind, your broker can work with you to find appropriate spaces. If you know your budget is $3,000, but you can't get the amount of space you need in town at that rent, your broker will know where you need to be. Maybe you'll get more space in the suburbs, or you can reduce your square footage in the main part of the city. Getting the variable of rent in place is a great starting point. Your broker will also help you be realistic with your budget. Chances are good that you won't be able to afford that full-floor penthouse downtown on a budget of only $5,000 per month.

You can set your budget, but there aren't set or standardized industry rental rates. Instead, there are general guidelines for different sectors. For example, restaurants like to keep their rental rates at approximately 6–7 percent of their gross revenue. Your gross revenue must be able to support the yearly rent before you sign the lease.

For example, if your restaurant is projected to bring in $100,000 per year, you would be able to afford only $7,000 per year in rent. Finding a space for $583 per month isn't realistic, so you should reconsider opening the restaurant.

Retail can withstand higher percentages of rent, up to 10 percent or 12 percent of gross revenue. Because other businesses vary in a multitude of ways, it's difficult to find a standard. For example, a call center might have gross revenues of $1 million and need twenty thousand square feet of space to house its employees. On the other end of the spectrum, a medical office might need only two thousand square feet of space but have revenues of $3 million. In these cases, rent that reflects a lower percentage of revenue is always better.

Your budget is also affected by the length of your lease. A long-term lease is a big commitment. If you are just starting out, it's in your best interest to pay a little more for a shorter term. A three-year lease is the norm, but you may be able to find a landlord willing to do a one year, or even month to month. Although you may be able to negotiate a shorter term lease, most landlords find them very unappealing.

Start small and work up to longer terms. Once you are

financially able to commit to longer leases, you will realize greater benefits. Landlords are happy to give a little more when they know they won't have to go to the trouble of leasing the space again for five or ten years.

Benefits of signing a longer term lease include free rent, lower rent, and build-out allowances.

Some types of businesses require longer leases in order to justify the expense of opening their doors. Restaurants may need a ten-year lease to recoup their investment in the build-out. Although it's more money spent through the term of the lease, landlords will give you more benefits in exchange for your willingness to stick around.

Another option is a five-year lease with extension options. You commit to five years, and if your business is going well, use your options for another five- or ten-year term. This type of lease will negate some of the risk and still allow you to stay where you are if things are going well.

Options benefit the tenant/business owner. Your broker can help you build them into your lease in the beginning. Then, if you decide to stay, the rent has already been pre-negotiated, so you know what your future expenses will be. If the market rent is lower, you can use this as leverage to renegotiate; if it's higher, you definitely want to stay.

This is particularly advantageous if the term is a long one that might otherwise be subject to rent increases or new tax assessments that would be passed on to the tenant.

Another negotiating point in the lease revolves around the build-out. When you need to make adjustments or improvements to the space you're leasing, either you or the landlord will have to pay for it. With a short-term lease, you'll probably be responsible for the full cost. When the term is longer, the landlord may be willing to help shoulder the expense. The build-out is basically an investment in your business, which a landlord won't be willing to make for the short term because they won't recoup their investment. Remember that the landlord is in business to make money, just like you are.

As you try to nail down your lease term, think about where you expect your business to be in six months, two years, and five years. Having smart goals in mind should drive your decisions. You wouldn't want to rent only eighteen hundred square feet if you plan on adding twenty new employees within the year. If you know you'll need to double your footprint, plan now for growth. Negotiate a shorter lease that you know you can get out of, or build in options or plans for expansion in the same building. Perhaps you can make sure you have a right to sublease, or you may be able to determine your growth trajectory and start out with a bigger space than you need right now. This is where a broker can help you make the determination and negotiate the best scenario to fit your circumstances.

CAUTION: PITFALLS FOR NEW LESSEES

There's a lot of excitement surrounding a move to a new space. You'll probably announce the move with colorful signage, have a grand opening, and get your name in the paper. Unfortunately, research shows that it usually takes about six months for substantially more traffic to come through your door.

Now you know, so make sure you have at least six months' worth of expenses set aside to cover your rent, payroll, inventory, and so on in the beginning. This is conservative, but it's better to be ready and be pleasantly surprised.

Although "planning for surprise" is an oxymoron, it's exactly what you must do. Hedge your bets. Things happen. Expensive things happen. Your lease will reduce your cash flow, so it's smart to be prepared financially to deal with issues that might pop up.

In addition to having savings set aside, you can also mitigate potential damages by being a smart negotiator before the lease is signed. One of the biggest potential expenses is the heating, ventilation, and air conditioning (HVAC) system. If the HVAC breaks, it could cost you $7,000-$12,000. Imagine agreeing to pay $1,500 in rent and then being forced to come up with another $10,000 to fix the HVAC only three months into the lease. Most small businesses couldn't take the hit—I've seen it happen.

Make sure all of the systems are inspected and in good condition before you take the property. If it's a second-generation space, meaning someone used it before you, there could be any number of hidden problems that would constitute major expenses totally unrelated to your business. Replacing a major system such as plumbing or electricity isn't in your normal business budget. It won't generate leads or make you money. If you can plan ahead for the problems that might occur, they won't affect you adversely.

NAVIGATING THE PROCESS

On the surface, the process of finding the right space seems easy enough. Decide what you're looking for, scout it out, and then purchase it or sign a lease. No big deal—just another do-it-yourself job. How hard could it be? Navigating the entire process the right way is actually much tougher than it appears, but the following tips will help you find the best commercial real estate deals on the market!

Technology
New technology can make your life much easier. Thanks to the internet, you can find and analyze deals from your couch, allowing you to view more properties than ever before. Staying on top of the new technology available isn't always a walk in the park, however, especially if it isn't your area of expertise. Although technology makes it easier for anyone to go online and search for properties with the characteristics they are seeking, it's also easier for others to manipulate those advances. I've seen brokers and owners market locations that aren't available so they can drum up more leads for other properties. This intentionally misleads prospects, and that's just the beginning!

What you see may not always be what you get. If you don't know the ins and outs of the commercial real estate business, you may find yourself in a deal that isn't what it appears to be. Although the internet can make your search more convenient, I strongly recommend that you always view a property in person before making an offer. Don't believe the pictures! You never know the true condition of the space until you see it for yourself.

Similarly, check out the area and neighboring businesses in person because they can also adversely affect the property's value. It seems like a no-brainer, but you'd be surprised at how many business owners will lease sight unseen (especially if moving from out of state).

Trends

As an entrepreneur anxious to start a new business or expand your current operations, it may be tempting to get caught up in the trends that are occurring in the real estate business. The right city, the right neighborhood, the right look—all of these things can be fashionable at certain times. It's important to understand that just because something is working for one business doesn't mean it's necessarily right for yours. Don't feel like you need to be in a certain area simply because that's where everyone is going. These trends tend to have a much higher price point due to their demand, and you may not need to spend that much money if it will only marginally increase your revenue.

Keep in mind, too, that you need to forecast the future of the area you're investigating and understand potential developments. If the city is planning on adding a greenway or closing two lanes on a five-lane road, it will impact your business!

Transactions

Real estate is full of transactions. You'll be dealing with discovery, property search, prospecting, workflow, verification, and tracking, just to name a few of the transactions that will take place. It's a big job for someone who knows what they're doing; for someone who doesn't, it would be very easy to let something important slip through the cracks.

When you're making an investment that could either kick start or kill your business's success, you have to know everything about the property. You don't want to find out two years down the road that there's an environmental issue that requires hundreds (yes, hundreds) of thousands of your own dollars to fix.

For an easy-to-navigate, eight-step info graphic of the commercial real estate process, see www.tylercauble.com/book.

THREE KEY POINTS

Looking for new real estate for your growing business can be very exciting. It's easy to get caught up in shiny new spaces and visions of what your business can accomplish. It's also easy to make mistakes. If you follow the tips in this chapter, you can avoid potential pitfalls and make the move with your business intact.

CONSULT YOUR ADVISERS

You're an expert in your business, not necessarily in finding a space or negotiating a lease. Just like you use an expert for accounting or information technology, there are also experts who can help you understand commercial real estate. Bring your advisers and commercial real estate broker into the process as early as possible. Their knowledge will be invaluable in areas where you have little experience.

DEFINE YOUR SPACE NEEDS

The best way to be successful in your property search is to know what you are looking for before you start. Having a real business need for more space is only the first step. The inquiry must also include the requirements of your new workspace and location, storage needs, and budget parameters. Writing down your precise needs currently and what they could be in the future gives you a checklist as you (and your broker) narrow down your possible choices.

THINK ABOUT LEASE LENGTH

The length of your lease is negotiable. Although it's great to be optimistic about the growth of your business, it pays to be smart regarding the time period you agree to stay in one location or pay a fixed amount of rent. Use your broker to help you understand options, build-outs, and kickout clauses. Realistically gauge where your business will be in six months, two years, and five years, and don't be afraid to start small and work up to a longer lease with better options.

ASSEMBLE YOUR A-TEAM

Although contemplating a move for your growing business is exciting, it can be overwhelming when the reality of actually finding the space sets in. But it doesn't have to be. There are specific steps you can follow to find the perfect place, and professionals who will make the process as seamless as possible.

FINDING A SPACE

So where is the best place to start? Whether you start with the old-fashioned drive-by or conduct an initial online search, finding the perfect space doesn't have to be difficult. You want to conduct your own due diligence with the end goal of finding the best commercial real estate broker to guide you through your journey.

THE DRIVE-BY SEARCH

The first thing you might do is drive around in the area you're interested in or conduct an online search. This can be time-consuming but beneficial if you note that most of the lease signs in your favorite area reference one particular broker. That broker might be one you want to talk to, especially because they seem to understand your market and have properties of interest to you. Like the residential real estate agent who seems to be representing every house in your favorite neighborhood, they obviously know the market and can help you find what's available.

REFERRAL TO A BROKER

If you'd rather save time and skip the drive-by search, getting a referral to a broker is your best option. Getting a referral is a quick and easy way to find out about a broker's expertise and how easy they are to work with.

For a referral to a qualified broker in your area, visit our website at www.tylercauble.com/book.

Business Contacts

Asking for referrals from your business contacts is a good idea regardless of the service you're seeking. You'll benefit from their mistakes because your friends and contacts won't refer you to anyone they don't trust, or anyone whose work is subpar.

Mentors or business coaches are another great referral source. Successful people know other successful people, and they're very good at networking. Ask questions, and chances are good that someone down the chain of referrals will introduce you to the right person to help.

Your business contacts and mentors have probably been in your shoes at least once. Find out how they found their space and ask about the broker they used. Once you have several referrals, interview at least three options. Get a few different viewpoints, learn how different brokers operate, and see where your personalities match up.

> For a list of questions to ask your broker, visit www.tylercauble.com/book.

Chamber of Commerce

Your local chamber of commerce is also a wealth of information. The chamber of commerce is typically made up of people who are very involved in their community and dedicated to being ethical business owners. It's safe to say that shady organizations will not last long in this environment.

The chamber provides a tremendous amount of value because they generally have strong memberships and they want to help. Members of the chamber are usually well trusted and have been around for a while, so they're the perfect group to poll regarding your new need for commercial real estate.

Join the chamber, attend the meetings, and start asking questions. Tell them you want to open up shop in a particular neighborhood and ask if they know anyone who could be helpful. You might also ask the following: Can you recommend a good commercial real estate broker? Have you used any good real estate attorneys lately? Can you refer me to a good contractor? All of these industries will be heavily represented in your local chamber of commerce.

Business Network International

Business Network International (BNI) is another group to mine for referrals. BNI is a leads group that has grown tremendously in recent years. It's similar to the chamber in that its members are business owners who meet to discuss business topics and for networking. Think of BNI as networking on steroids. In each BNI chapter, only one industry is allowed per chair, so they are scrutinized before they are accepted.

Each member in a BNI group is vetted by the whole, because everyone wants their group to be robust. The members of each chapter learn about the other industries in the group and essentially become a sales force for them.

You can leverage the knowledge and skills of the BNI group in your area. Attend a meeting as a visitor, or call the BNI regional office to get a list of commercial brokers within all of the chapters near you. They love to pass referral information to anyone who needs it, and you don't have to be a member to take advantage of that service.

Residential Real Estate Agent

Your residential real estate agent can be used as a referral source, but don't fall into the trap of asking them to represent you in the commercial context. The agent who sold you a home may have a good commercial broker contact to share with you, but they probably don't have the expertise you need in that area. You wouldn't hire an attorney specializing in mergers and acquisitions if you got into a car wreck, right?

Unfortunately, business owners who don't understand the vast differences between residential and commercial will get burned when they let their residential agent help them find business space. Consider the tenant who decided not to renew and asked their residential agent to find them a bigger place. Their lease was set to expire March 31, so the landlord found another tenant to move in on April 1. As expected, the residential agent was unable to find them any suitable properties. A week before their lease expired, they had nowhere to go, and they no longer had the option to hold over because a new tenant was moving in.

The residential agent simply didn't have the contacts or resources to find the available properties. Similarly, it wouldn't be smart to ask your commercial broker to find your new home. Commercial brokers typically don't have access to the MLS, don't know where to find residential buyers, and know nothing about staging a house for a quick sale. It's unfamiliar territory.

LANDLORDS AND TENANTS

Your previous landlord might also be a source of good information about other spaces that are available that might suit your needs. They might have another tenant moving out of a suitable property, and they usually know other property owners and can point you in the right direction. They won't mind helping you if they know they don't have anything else to offer and you're already on the way out.

If you've settled on the area you want to be in, I recommend you talk to the current tenants in that shopping center or office building. See if anyone is trying to sublet their property, or ask them for the landlord's contact information. Current tenants can also provide helpful information regarding the foot traffic, how the landlord conducts his business, typical maintenance issues, and so on. Just by talking to people in the know, you will gain knowledge and learn of different opportunities.

THE RIGHT PROFESSIONAL FOR THE JOB

In any complex business transaction, the smart business owner knows the importance of having appropriate counsel who specializes in the matter at hand. Commercial real estate transactions are no different.

All real estate is not created equally. There are distinct industry specialties and agents to help you who have specific expertise. Just as you wouldn't want a plastic surgeon to handle your brain surgery, choosing the right agent for the job will help you avoid the potential issues related to the differing markets and types of negotiation.

Although residential real estate agents are allowed by law to facilitate commercial leases, the skill set required is very different. Most residential agents won't have access to all of the commercial listings and won't be fluent in commercial lease terms, build-outs, and all of the ways to protect a small business tenant. Residential agents have good intentions. They want to serve their clients in any way possible, but I can't tell you how many times I've seen businesses suffer because an inexperienced broker found and negotiated their deal.

According to Inman News, the leading news source for the real estate industry, the most common ways real estate agents get sued relate directly to the problem of participating in transactions they are unqualified to handle. The list includes:

1. Failure to disclose a property defect

2. Breach of duty

3. Representing clients in unfamiliar territory

4. Providing misleading information

5. Not protecting the client

6. Negligence

It's possible for all of these issues to arise when the professional you choose to handle your deal doesn't specialize in the appropriate area. Use a residential real estate agent when you buy a house, but rely on a commercial broker to guide you through finding a property and the minefield of negotiating the lease. It's best to spend your time finding the right professional on the front end instead of having to sue them on the back end for damages due to inexperience.

ADVANTAGES OF WORKING WITH A BROKER

Once you find the commercial broker you want to work with, you will realize all of the benefits of having an expert in your corner. By virtue of working in the field, an experienced commercial broker will know the market through and through. He can help you meet your goals while staying true to your budget.

While you're taking care of business, your broker can handle the grunt work associated with vetting a property and negotiating a lease. Instead of having to call every possible option, set up appointments and view, and then make a decision based on the comps, your broker will narrow your choices without your presence and bring you in to see the best options. The broker finds the space; you sit back and relax.

After you choose a property, the negotiation begins, and this is where the broker's knowledge is particularly helpful. Commercial leases are nothing like residential leases. Every commercial lease is different and almost everything is negotiable. Brokers know market value and can help you determine fair rent, as well as who will be responsible for specific costs associated with the space.

Commercial brokers are generally paid like residential agents. Instead of making the small business owner pay for representation, the landlord is responsible for paying the broker's fee. This style of compensation is especially helpful to small business owners—you have enough expenses to worry about! Similar to residential agents who can represent either a buyer or a seller, the commercial broker can represent a landlord and have property listings, they can represent the tenant, or they can represent both parties.

Neither type of broker works for free, but the landlord is always the one paying the fee. In other words, your broker knows the market, will help you find a site, negotiate on your behalf, keep pulling everything in the right direction, and it won't cost you anything.

In fact, using a knowledgeable broker will usually *save* you money. A broker can review the lease and cover the big points with you while saving you the time of diving into the small and generally unimportant issues. He will explain the lease to you and make the applicable changes before sending it to your attorney. It's a free service by the broker that means you only pay your attorney for the final review.

Brokers are also familiar with all of the little things in a lease that can end up costing you the most. Commercial leases can be extremely long (and extremely boring), so having a broker who understands the minutiae will help tremendously.

As previously discussed, many leases are written in the landlord's favor, so why wouldn't they try to put responsibility for such items as the HVAC unit on the tenant? This one sentence in a thirty-page contract can cost you $10,000 if you aren't careful. It seems innocuous, but what if that unit is twelve years old and blows out five months into your lease? Most new businesses would be unable to handle such a large outlay of cash—especially for a fixture that you're buying on behalf of the landlord.

The restaurant industry illustrates another example of how a broker's experience pays off in real dollars. Restaurants usually require some degree of construction, during which time you can negotiate a period of free rent. It wouldn't be smart to make payments before you open your doors. There's a reason it's called dead rent. However, you can't start construction until the landlord provides the necessary documents, such as as-builts and construction drawings for the space.

An experienced broker would make sure the lease states that the period of free rent begins tolling only *after* these documents are received. Otherwise, your free rent period could be up before the landlord ever gives you what you need for the build-out. One sentence changes everything, but only if there is experience in the room that knows what that sentence is.

FINDING A TRUSTWORTHY BROKER

Turning over such a big decision to someone you don't know very well can be unnerving. Finding a broker through a referral from a colleague can set you at ease, because you can trust your acquaintance's experience with them. It's also a good idea to talk to former clients of the broker and get references to learn how the broker treated and worked for other businesses.

Make sure your broker is familiar with the type of space you require. Ask him for his most recent clients who were in a situation similar to yours to see how they handled the situation. Call them and ask the hard questions, then trust your gut. Most brokers are ethical and will have your best interests at heart, but there are always exceptions. It's good to know whom you're working with.

THE BROKER-CLIENT AGREEMENT

When you find a broker whom you like and trust, it's recommended that you sign a broker-client agreement. This document details the fiduciary relationship between you and your broker and serves as the contract for representation, not to mention that it's what the broker takes to the landlord to get paid.

EXCLUSIVITY

When you enter into an agreement with one broker, you are giving him the exclusive right to find a property, negotiate on your behalf, and get paid for his services. Although you may think it's better to have many brokers searching for properties for you, it's in your best interest to work with only one. Brokers are only paid if they find a property for you, and without an exclusive arrangement, there's no motivation to work on your behalf.

No broker wants to work with someone who wants to work with everyone else. Think of it like a personal relationship. Once there is commitment, most people aren't OK with their significant other shopping around for other prospects. Your relationship with your broker is similar. Why would a broker take the risk of doing all the work to send you properties when there is a chance you could take it straight to the landlord or another broker? When you commit to one broker and sign his agreement, you are essentially hiring someone who is dedicated to finding you exactly what you are looking for. They will immediately go to work because they know the landlord will eventually reimburse them for their time.

EXPIRATION DATE

In order to be a legal contract, the broker-client agreement must have an expiration date. This date is negotiable, but a good rule of thumb is one year and then month to month thereafter.

Another way to protect yourself is to have a bilateral cancellation clause so either party can get out of the contract with thirty days' notice in writing. Although you would no longer be under contract going forward, you aren't allowed to lease any of the properties shown to you by the broker for a certain period of time depending on your state laws, unless you or the landlord pay his commission. It's a fair way to handle the responsibilities under the agreement.

SCOPE OF WORK

The agreement with the broker should also include the scope of work you are hiring him to do. Make it specific, not open ended. You want to carefully define the type of property you're looking for in terms of square footage, budget, category of space (warehouse, industrial, retail, office, etc.), and geographical area. Don't worry if you aren't sure about some of the variables. The scope of work is something that may change as you go, but thinking it through at this stage will give your broker a good place to start.

COMMISSION

The representation agreement also covers the fee arrangement acknowledging that the landlord is responsible for the commission. To be safe, there should be nothing in the agreement that leaves you responsible for paying the broker if the landlord refuses to cover it.

Although you're not on the hook for commission, you should be ready to back up your broker with the landlord should it be necessary. In other words, be willing to walk from the property if the landlord doesn't want to pay. Landlords who refuse to pay broker fees don't stay in business very long because brokers won't bring tenants their way. If they aren't willing to follow the codes of commercial real estate, there's no telling what they'll try to pull over on you.

REAL ESTATE PROFESSIONALS YOU WILL NEED

In addition to a broker, your most important resource, there are other real estate professionals who will be important to you. Good brokers will be tied in to the real estate community in your area and can assist you as your needs arise. Brokers often use the same professionals for all of their deals and they know who can be counted on to deliver quality work on time, and who you will want to avoid.

REAL ESTATE ATTORNEY

Regardless of the type of property or size of the deal, you'll need an attorney to review the legal documents. Your broker can suggest a real estate attorney who's good at bringing the parties together and making deals happen, as opposed to the majority who try to find everything wrong with a deal and bill you all along the way.

You should be able to have an attorney review everything for a flat fee, depending on the size of the contract. Although your broker isn't allowed to give legal advice, they can make recommendations on the lease. However, you can't just take a broker's word for it. You must have an attorney review the contract. You'll save attorney's fees if your broker makes the preliminary changes and delivers the lease to the attorney for final review. Attorneys are very good at thinking through everything that could possibly go wrong. It's much better to spend $500 to catch a mistake now that could cost you $10,000 later.

BUILDING INSPECTOR

Always have your space inspected before you sign a lease. Although doing so is more important in a second-generation space (one that has been occupied before), even new spaces should be inspected. In many multistory office leases, the landlord will typically take all responsibility in a full-service gross (FSG) lease, and inspections won't be as important. But if you're taking a ground-floor retail or office on any sort of net lease, you'll want to know for what, exactly, you're accepting responsibility.

A building inspector will examine the mechanical, electrical, and plumbing systems and prepare a report covering everything from the crawl space to the roof. You can use the report in your negotiation with the landlord and to help plan the space to fit your needs.

Everything must be up to code. Owners or previous tenants often try to fix things themselves with disastrous consequences, particularly in the electrical system. In an older space, the wiring may not have been touched for fifty years and will need to be repaired to get up to code. Take building codes seriously. All it takes is a lightning strike without surge protectors for an older building to go up in flames.

The most important mechanical element to be checked out is the HVAC system. If it's lost during your tenancy and you have to replace it, the expense will undoubtedly be more than you want to bear. Most systems will last from twelve to fifteen years, so make sure you know the age and the condition before moving forward.

Plumbing includes the toilets, sinks, faucets, dishwashers,

drains, and so forth and can also become a big expense. Plumbing is hidden for the most part, so you really don't know what's happening without a thorough inspection.

A good building inspector is worth the price you'll pay for his expertise. He'll save you money by making recommendations that you can have the landlord fix before you take control of the property. It's always better to have a complete picture of your new space, for better or worse. Once you know where you stand, you can better plan for the future.

GENERAL CONTRACTOR

Finding a general contractor (GC) for your build-out doesn't have to be difficult, but spending some time will be worth it if you can find a good one. Again, brokers work with contractors routinely and can provide referrals, as well as handle the relationship if needed.

Make sure your GC has the reputation for completing jobs on time and that he pulls the permits necessary for the scope of work. He can also help you plan the space and make sure everything is built to code.

Unfortunately, not all GCs are created equal. For example, consider the professional office in the suburbs that decided to open a complementary service next door to their main location. The GC hired to do the work charged $100,000 to build out two thousand square feet. Not only was the client overcharged for the work desired, but also the work itself was terrible—they didn't even have outlets or overhead lights in the private rooms. The GC wouldn't respond to the business owner's complaints and refused to fix the issues, and the owner eventually had to abandon the space and put the $100,000 in the loss column.

You can avoid problems like this with a little due diligence and good advice from your broker and business contacts. Also, never hire a GC who solicits by going door to door or pressures you to make a quick decision. Be leery of anyone requiring that you pay for the entire job up front or who takes cash only as a payment. The type of GC you hire is also critical in avoiding potential complications.

Just as there are different types of real estate agents, there are also residential and commercial contractors. Commercial contractors follow different codes and use different materials. For example, if you use residential flooring in a commercial setting, it's not going to last with all the clients and employees coming through the door. Commercial-grade flooring is made to withstand heavier traffic and more intense wear and should last at least five years. Commercial contractors are aware of your special needs and will build to suit them.

QUESTIONS TO ASK BEFORE HIRING A GENERAL CONTRACTOR

Selecting the right contractor for your job is important to your success. Unfortunately, there are some bad contractors, but there are also some excellent ones who will give you professional results at a fair price. So how can you be sure you are making the right choice?

The key is in asking questions and interviewing candidates who have been recommended to you. It doesn't have to be a guessing game. Check the Better Business Bureau and ask your family, friends, and broker to give you the names of good contractors, and then conduct your own due diligence. A few questions to ask include:

- Do you have a license and insurance? Make sure the GC can show you up-to-date credentials, including a contractor's license that is valid in your state. Always make sure the GC has general liability and workman's compensation insurance.

- Have you done this type of project before? How recently? Can I see your portfolio? Find out if he's up on the latest developments in the business.

- What does your quote include? Is it a fixed price or an estimate? Get an itemized list of what's included in the quote, including details of all materials to be used. Make sure you understand what happens if unexpected issues occur.

- How long will it take you to do this job? What's your projected time line, and how does the payment schedule fit with that? Ask for a clear time line of project milestones and payments.

- What kind of warranty on labor and materials comes with the project?

- Who is responsible for pulling the required building permits?

For more questions to ask when interviewing a contractor, please visit www.tylercauble.com/book.

THE BROKER-CLIENT RELATIONSHIP

Your broker is the most important tool in your real estate toolbox. A good one will want to continue the relationship with you even after you close the deal. Think of your broker as your own real estate department.

When you have real estate needs or concerns, call on your broker to help. You can concentrate on your business and let your broker help you in their area of expertise. Questions regarding your lease will pop up from time to time, and your broker is available to provide the answers. Often, brokers are willing to help you with your build-out and continue to make referrals when needs such as carpet cleaning or IT issues arise.

If you chose well, you will have a strong relationship with your broker. Let him help you, and you can return the favor the next time you're in the market for a new place to hang up your business sign.

THREE KEY POINTS

Moving from an idea to a new business space can be an overwhelming task, but not if you assemble an A-team to help you.

FOCUS ON YOUR BUSINESS

As outlined in the introduction, an important step in the process of finding and leasing a space is to focus on your business. Looking at real estate can be addictive. It's fun and exciting to find spaces and dream about the future. However, it's also extremely time-consuming, and there's no way for you to know about all of the sources of potential listings. It doesn't make sense to spend all of your time and energy on the hunt, particularly if it's to the detriment of your business.

The point of hiring a real estate broker is to leverage their experience and knowledge in numerous ways so you can concentrate on what's most important—your business.

Let your team do what they are best at, so you can do your job as well.

ASK FOR REFERRALS

Referrals are a business owner's best friend. Whether you're searching for the best coffee or the best contractor, ask around and take advantage of the experiences of others. Take advantage of mistakes that others have made so you don't make the same ones.

Ask mentors, friends, relatives, associations, and your broker for advice and referrals to other professionals you'll need. Pay particular attention if the same names keep popping up. Interview several potentials before making a choice. Trust the referrals and trust your intuition and you are much less likely to get burned.

PROFESSIONALS SAVE YOU MONEY

It's tempting to cut corners, especially at a time when you need cash to run your business. Maybe you want to get by without an attorney or ask your handy brother-in-law to check out the property instead of hiring an inspector. Don't do it! Hiring experienced professionals will save you money in the long run.

Spend now to save later. There's a reason your broker recommends a professional inspection. Chances are he's seen what happens when the business owner doesn't know all of the potential pitfalls inherent in the property. Similarly, attorneys and other real estate professionals are there to protect you. Arm yourself with professionals who will make sure you know what you're getting into, and you'll face fewer surprises during your tenancy.

3

COMPARE POTENTIAL
SPACES

As discussed in the last chapter, finding a space might involve driving around in neighborhoods that you're interested in, calling landlords, getting referrals, and hiring a broker. The time it takes to find the right place for your business to call home is dependent on your space requirements and the state of the market where you want to be. It may take a few days, or it may take months, but by planning ahead, you can make the process more efficient.

Not every space you see will be ideal, but it's helpful to look at the variety of spaces that your broker finds for you. Doing so will give you an idea of what is actually out there in the market as well as a solid baseline to start from. So the next steps are to tour your sites and weigh your options. It's your broker's job to bring you qualified properties. You don't want to be in the position of looking at only one space and getting into a bidding war with other potential tenants. No one but the landlord will win in that situation. Keep your options open so you have something for comparison and don't get backed into a corner.

In an ideal world, your broker would show you at least six properties that he has vetted according to your requirements and the scope of work in your agreement. Unfortunately, depending on your specific needs and the current market climate, that may not be possible, but anything is better than just one. Tour all of the properties in one day if you can. Your options will stay fresh in your mind if you can see them back to back, which will help you best compare each property.

Another reason to tour all of the properties at the same time is because it enables you to move quickly. You can lose a property that could work for you to another tenant if you're waiting around to see other spaces before you make a decision. Your ability to move quickly is crucial if the real estate market is hot. In these markets, some properties receive bids as soon as they're listed. Even in a down market, your ability to move quickly could give you an advantage on pricing or earn you other concessions from the landlord, because they'll see you as well organized and professional. If you know you're ready to move, don't waste time.

The faster you act, the more likely you are to get the property you want and avoid a bidding war. In a landlord-friendly market, the landlord receives the benefit of having lots of options. If your offer is late or not the most attractive, you may have a tougher time landing in the spot you want to be.

On the other hand, you have all the power as a tenant in a down market, so you and your broker should approach the negotiations as such. Consider the beauty supply store that signed their lease in 2010 in a very down market. Because they knew the corridor they were situated on was where they wanted to be long term, they took advantage of the market climate and locked in a long-term lease at a very low rate. Now that the market has rebounded, rents on this corridor have more than quadrupled, but the beauty supply store continues to pay next to nothing. It pays to hit the market at the right time!

CONSIDERATIONS WHEN COMPARING SPACES

Once you tour the handful of options the broker has for you, try to narrow them down to three. This is somewhat of an intuitive process because you can rely on your gut feeling, but you also need to compare the tangible attributes of each property: financial costs, traffic, visibility, and so forth. You should have no problem picking the top contenders because you set guidelines with your broker before you began the search. It gets a little trickier from this point on, but using a checklist with the following considerations will help.

LOCATION

Location is the name of the game in real estate. Your customers will not be able find you if you're in a bad location, or even a good one that lacks visibility. Recruiting strong talent to work for you will also be difficult if the commute or even parking situation is less than ideal. Location also takes other things into consideration, some of which we discussed in earlier chapters but deserve a mention here:

1. Co-tenancy: Are you surrounded by complementary businesses or competitive businesses? Depending on your industry, either might work for you. For example, fast food restaurants actually share their revenue numbers with one another because they find it beneficial to be near other fast food restaurants. A nail salon, however, is a unique business and probably doesn't want to be next to another nail salon, where they could

cannibalize each other's business. If your business is unique, look for a neighborhood where there is a void in the type of product or services you provide.

2. Employee considerations: The availability of labor in your area is a valid concern before you sign a lease. If your business centers on manufacturing or fulfillment, you may need to locate where there is a strong blue-collar population, perhaps somewhere more rural. Consider the availability of public transportation and how convenient your location might be to the bus or train stop. One of the biggest commercial real estate agencies in the world, CBRE, recently conducted a study for Bridgestone who was considering moving away from Nashville, Tennessee. CBRE did a competitive analysis of the five or six cities that Bridgestone was considering and determined that the core group of employees interested in working at Bridgestone would prefer to live in Nashville as opposed to San Francisco, New York, Dallas, or Atlanta. It was unanimous, and Bridgestone knew they would have a better chance of finding and keeping the most educated employees if they stayed where they were.

3. Neighborhoods with your clientele: Put your business where your clients already are. Find a location that is convenient to your target consumer, and oftentimes they'll reward you for doing so. If your clientele is north of downtown, why would you want to be south

of downtown? Seems very straightforward, right? But many businesses don't even think about it. Another consideration is whether customers come to you or if you take your services to them. Choose a neighborhood that makes it easy for you and your customers to find each other. Convenience is key.

4. Near suppliers: If you are dependent on specific suppliers, it may be cost-effective to be close to them. If you run out of products or supplies, how quickly can you restock? Can you drive over and pick it up, or does it have to be shipped? Similarly, consider your proximity to the interstate and if it's important to you, your employees, or your customers.

5. Zoning: Typically, a tenant doesn't have to worry too much about zoning. However, if you need an office or retail space, you'll want to go where the area is zoned for offices or retail operations. I saw an unrepresented retail business lease a building that was zoned for office, only to find out they couldn't operate their business in that location after investing tens of thousands into retrofitting the building. Trust your broker to show you appropriately zoned properties, but also make sure in your lease that the landlord represents and warrants that the location is zoned for your intended use.

6. Parking: Does the potential space have enough parking to accommodate your customers immediately? Or will they be required to drive around and wait for a space

to open up? If you're in an area where customers are used to pulling up and parking right outside, they will avoid you if you don't offer that convenience. Another consideration is parking for your employees. No one wants to park down the street and walk a block or two to their office, unless you are in a city with advanced public transportation and the workforce is used to that style of commute.

7. Image: Does your new space match the image you want to convey? For example, if you sell luxury goods, you'll want to stay in the high-end part of town with impeccable finishes on both the interior and exterior. A spa in a blue-collar neighborhood won't be as successful as one in a more extravagant neighborhood. Pay attention to your demographics and cater to them. You may have to pay a little more for a more prestigious address, but it will be worth it in the long run.

8. Neighborhood: Similar to the image consideration, some neighborhoods specifically suit certain types of businesses due to the habits of local residents. Your broker will be helpful in knowing where they are and how it could affect you. For example, would you locate your new restaurant in a suburb with little office space where the lunch traffic would be nonexistent? Although you might get cheaper rent farther out, it might be worth paying the extra freight to be within a one-mile radius of the city center where there are

potentially hundreds of thousands of employees who need to find a bite at noon. Run the cost-benefit analysis and figure out what makes the most sense for you.

ECONOMICS OF THE LEASE

The economics of the lease include everything related to the financial impact of the deal in the offer you make to the landlord. These are the things that must be considered as you compare your top three choices. At the most basic level, you should compare the cost per square foot, the cost of utilities, the pass-throughs (your common area expenses, taxes, and insurance), and build-out. Ask your broker to lead you through a comparison of all of the properties based on the bottom line of what it will cost you to be in each particular space.

Other important aspects to compare are the cost of build-out and possibility of free rent during that time. If one space offers to pay for your build-out and offers free rent during construction, leasing that space becomes much more attractive than a similar space where you pay all of the expenses.

Although not a literal financial item like rent, there are other considerations in the lease that can affect your bottom line. For example, you need to determine if you will be granted exclusive use. Are you going to be the only yoga studio allowed in the shopping center, or is there a chance the landlord would let another one locate next door? You always want to negotiate for exclusive use, and if you can't get it, perhaps that is a mark against that property in your comparison. While not absolutely necessary for your business, exclusive uses certainly do mitigate your risk.

You also want to negotiate for a subletting option. It will be important as you grow, and perhaps even more important if your business fails. If you aren't making the money to pay your rent, you want to make sure you have the right to find someone who can. I would advise against signing any lease that doesn't allow you to sublease the property; it's just too risky. Most leases will allow subleasing with the landlord's permission.

Finally, make sure you understand the differences in what you are required to do under the lease of each property, and who is paying for additional property expenses. If you're in an office building, you may be under a full-service lease, which means your rent is all-inclusive. The landlord handles all of the other expenses. In this situation, you wouldn't face any monthly surprises. Leases for retail space are typically triple net leases, where the tenant pays for taxes, insurance, and common area maintenance (the three nets) in addition to rent. You can't make a true comparison of properties until you understand the economics and responsibilities of each one and how they differ.

AVAILABILITY

Market availability in your area is an important consideration, particularly if your needs are unique and the option you desire is rare to come by. Availability may weigh heavily in your decision making if you know that a particular space may not be on the market again for a very long time. It's best to begin your search 180 days prior to your needing to be in a space. If your needs are difficult to accommodate, this should give you enough time to find a space and get everything together.

If a real estate product is not readily available in your market, your negotiation will be different than the negotiation for a property that is easy to find. There is not as much room for getting what you want, the negotiation will be tougher, and you have to move fast. However, this situation could work to your advantage. If a space is tough to come by, that means there is a smaller market looking for that product, so you may be one of the few people the landlord talks to with regard to the space.

POTENTIAL FOR GROWTH

Potential for growth refers to the growth in the neighborhood, but also refers to whether the space allows for the growth of your business. Will you have the option to expand your office if needed? Can you move to a bigger spot in the same building without penalty? You don't want to sign a five-year deal only to realize two years into it that you've hired too many people and need to move. Now you either have to buy out of your lease or find a subtenant to assume your responsibilities, neither of which you'll want to deal with.

THE BEST DEAL

When comparing properties, most business owners want to know which one is the best deal. This is a composite of all of the points of consideration but is also very subjective to you and your business. What's the best location? Who is giving the most free rent and paying for the most build-out? When everything is thrown into the mix, which property is the most attractive?

WHY THERE ARE FOUR GAS STATIONS ON THE SAME STREET

Have you ever wondered why Home Depot always opens near Lowe's, or why all of the fast food restaurants are in the same part of town? It's called competitive clustering, and it's no accident.

Competition requires businesses to locate where they can capture the largest possible share of the market. Because they want to be centrally located to their customer, it follows that the central location would be the same for similar businesses. It makes sense for comparable businesses to cluster together instead of seeking out a dedicated market area. I like to call this the water-hole effect.

Competitive clustering might make sense for your business, especially if you have goods or services that are routinely consumed and your competitors are already in the same place. It may not make as much difference and could actually harm you if you are a unique business or if brand plays a big role in determining consumer choice. For instance, a chiropractor opening up next door to a chiropractor could be devastating to both businesses because of how specialized their services are.

Studies have shown that there's power in numbers, and that two or three businesses sharing the same area will do better as a whole than if they were isolated. Consumers appreciate the variety and choice, and it allows them to shop and compare products and services. When like businesses colocate, more people are drawn into the area and more business is generated.

NEW BUILDINGS VERSUS SECOND-GENERATION BUILDINGS

In both new buildings and buildings that previously housed tenants, you have the opportunity to build the space out to fit your needs. New buildings are typically bare bones and may only have four walls and a door. Although you'll have to create your space from the ground up, everything will be new. You'll get to choose the floor plan, the finishes, and everything else about the space to make it your own. Many businesses love the opportunity new construction presents, because they get to design their office to be the most effective and efficient for their needs. If you can wait for the space to be built out, which is typically 60–120 days depending on your needs, it's well worth it.

In a second-generation property, the space will often reflect the former tenant's needs. You won't have as many options for change, or it will require more work to rearrange the space at the very least, but you also won't have the greater expense of starting from scratch. If you have a business that requires a certain kind of look, the second-generation space might not be the best option unless you can negotiate tenant improvements with the landlord. A space planner or designer may come in handy at this point, because they can take a current floor plan and show you what it could be after you've rearranged and finished construction.

The finishes in each potential building are also something to consider. In a second-generation space, you may only have the option of building standard selections for paint and carpet. The landlord knows his numbers and won't deviate too far from standard finishes. If you're building out a brand-new space, you may have an allowance for the build-out and be able to choose any finishes within your budget. Standard finishes, however, aren't always limited by price. The spaces will have to be painted and carpeted again by the next tenant, so it's important that they can be easily finished over. Having a consistent look is also paramount to maintaining a professional commercial property.

One of your most important considerations when comparing new and second-generation properties is whether the space is up to code. While codes are generally not an issue with new buildings, you have to be careful with older spaces. The electrical systems may be forty years old, or the HVAC might be located next to a gas pipe. Codes today are very different than they were years ago, which means there may be extra expenses associated with becoming code compliant.

Similarly, the Americans with Disabilities Act (ADA) didn't become law until 1990. Buildings constructed before this time won't always have the required access. If your business is open to the general public, you can't discriminate against anyone with a disability, and access must be provided. Before you decide on a second-generation space, determine whether you or your landlord is responsible for making the building accessible. However, if you aren't pulling permits or performing any work in the space, the property could be grandfathered in and won't require updating. It's best to rely on your broker and attorney in this case.

WHAT TO DO IF YOU FIND A POTENTIAL PROSPECT

When working with a broker, avoid the temptation to call the landlord yourself and see a space that you'd like to know more about. Let your broker know—that's what he's there for. You don't want to call the landlord and have to explain after the fact that there's a broker involved who will be negotiating on your behalf and collecting fees for his services from the property owner. Landlords don't like finding out after a discussion with a tenant that they're on the hook for commission but have no problems paying commissions if they have always dealt with the broker. It's better to work through the channels you already have in place and not get into that uncomfortable position to begin with. After all, that's what you've hired your broker to do on your behalf.

If you must call the landlord yourself, tell him early on in your conversation that you're represented and all communications going forward will be through your broker. Landlords will be amenable to the situation as long as they know up front what the deal looks like.

If you fail to reveal that you are represented to the landlord, you may end up having to pay your broker. Or the broker may back out if he's not going to be paid, and you'll end up negotiating alone or having to hire a costly real estate attorney to do basic negotiations for you. It's easy to save yourself the drama. Keep everyone in the loop and the deal will go smoothly.

THREE KEY POINTS

Comparing your top choices is the only way to know which property will meet your needs. Let your broker take you on a tour of properties on a single day, if possible, and then guide you through the best points of comparison.

VISITING MULTIPLE SITES

The only way to know what's going to work for you is to visit multiple sites and find out what you like and what you don't. Your broker will find as many properties as he can that match your requirements, then he'll show you the ones that are the best fit. You should tour as many sites as possible in one day.

CONTROLLING YOUR EMOTIONS

Enthusiasm is a great quality once you've decided on a space, but it's not going to help you during negotiation if the landlord knows how much you love it and *have to have it*. Stay neutral while viewing properties in the presence of the landlord or his representative. Save your true feeling to share with your broker at a later date. Let the landlord do a little work to gain your interest.

MAKING THE COMPARISON

Once you have toured the prospective spaces and made some notes, it's time to narrow down your options. The initial cut is the easiest. You should have a pretty good idea of properties that just won't work. With the remaining options, make a comparison based on location, economics, availability, and growth. When you have the numbers and facts in front of you, the best deal will emerge, and you're ready to move to the next stage of the process.

PART TWO

NEGOTIATING
THE LEASE

4

GIVE-AND-TAKE

You've finally found the perfect spot. Let the negotiations begin! The first step after finding your new location is to draft a letter of intent (LOI). The LOI describes the economics of the deal and serves as your proposal to the landlord. Depending on the landlord's preferences, they may draft the LOI on their form to open the conversation. Either way, it won't matter because you'll be negotiating for what you'd like to have.

All of the relevant and important factors that will eventually go in the lease are covered in the LOI. For example, you'll establish the parties and identify the space and square footage, as well as discuss the term and financial details.

The LOI is intended to be brief, usually two or three pages, as opposed to the twenty or thirty pages of a full lease. The goal is to provide a starting point to negotiate the deal. Why take the extra step of negotiating an LOI when you could cut straight to the chase with a lease? Well, because many leases can be detailed and thorough, there's no need for both parties to get attorneys involved and working on a lease draft if they can't come to terms on the base rent, tenant improvements, and so forth.

At this point, your broker should have prepared you to include your financials with the LOI to show the landlord you can back up your offer. Hopefully, you started pulling them together when you decided to look for a space and already have the package assembled. Think of it like buying a new home—the buyer who has pre-approval will be the successful one, especially in a hot market. Many sellers won't even consider offers unless the potential buyer has been preapproved, and commercial is no different. Having your financials ready, and providing them up front, shows that you are prepared and should be taken seriously.

The process can differ slightly if your broker signifies your interest to the landlord and asks him to provide the first offer. In this case, it's sometimes called a request for proposal (RFP). Regardless of who provides the first proposal, it's nonbinding and there are no attorneys involved. The LOI and the RFP simply represent a good place to start.

The LOI is not a lease and doesn't come with any guarantees of securing the property. Even if you've come to terms on an LOI and all parties have executed it, it doesn't mean the space is necessarily reserved for you and your business. You still have to negotiate and come to terms on the finer points in a formal lease. This can work in your favor when there is high demand for properties that fit your needs, because you can offer an LOI on several different properties at the same time. It's wise to not put all of your eggs in one basket, because whichever business comes to agreeable terms on a lease with the landlord and executes first will win the space.

When there's a lot of competition, it pays to act fast on all of the properties you like. It's not uncommon to begin negotiating an LOI only to be notified by the landlord that the space is no longer available. The landlord can accept more than one LOI on the same property. Wouldn't you do the same if you wanted to have the best chance of leasing property you owned? He may have even executed several LOIs on the property you want, and everyone may be negotiating simultaneously. I can't stress enough that the first party to finish negotiations and sign the lease will secure the space.

THE LETTER OF INTENT

Now that we've laid the groundwork for negotiations, what is actually covered in an LOI? The LOI demonstrates to the landlord that you want the property and you're serious about taking the steps to lease it. Again, it's not an official contract. The LOI is merely a recitation of the main points of the deal that form the basis for the lease agreement.

The LOI includes specific information, but it's a straightforward and often simple document. The LOI should include:

1. Name of the tenant and business: most small businesses are filed as an LLC, which could be dissolved overnight. Landlords will protect their interests by having the owners of the company sign as the tenant with a DBA (Doing Business As) to follow.
2. Name of the landlord.
3. Address and size of the space to be leased: typically referred to as the premises, but this could vary depending on location, landlord, and so forth.
4. Intended use and any related use (e.g., nail salon that sells beauty products).
5. Base rent and additional charges: Base rent will differ depending on whether the space is retail or in an office building. *Additional charges* is a technical term referring to charges beyond the base rate that have to be

paid in order to keep the space open. This section references the type of lease you will have, such as full service, modified gross, triple net, and so forth.

6. Scope of work: What kind of build-out is required, and who is responsible for the expense?

7. Possession date upon fully executed lease: The possession date may be different from the date your rent starts due to the build-out required to get the property ready.

8. Commencement of rent: If you are doing a build-out, you don't want to be paying rent until you can open your doors and occupy the space. Ask for rent abatement and include it in your offer. Thirty to ninety days is typically the time allowed for a build-out in an office or retail building. Restaurants generally require 120–150 days.

9. Security deposit.

10. Signage permitted on site: Do you require large signs, or will a minimal decal work? Make sure the requirements of the building or area match the signage you prefer.

11. Financial statements: The agreement is usually contingent on a review of the tenant's financials. Most landlords will not waste their time negotiating the LOI until they know the tenant is able to meet the financial demands of the deal.

For a template of a letter of intent, please visit www.tylercauble.com/leasing-tips.

The LOI is nonbinding, which should be stated on the document to prevent any confusion, and you can walk away from the deal without penalty at any time. It's truly a formality to negotiating the lease and will save both parties time and money. This might be viewed as a nuisance because you aren't guaranteed the property, but the benefit is that you show the landlord why they should take you seriously.

There are two additional clauses that the savvy business owner should include in the LOI. First, always negotiate free rent, often called rent abatement. Most likely, the landlord isn't going to suggest it, but they will usually agree to free rent for some period of time if you have good credit and the length of the deal is long enough for them to recapture their costs.

Second, if it is necessary in your business to be the only member of that industry practicing on the property, ask for an exclusivity clause. If you're a dentist, you may not want other dentists in your building competing with you for the same clientele. However, if you're an attorney or accounting firm, it won't matter as much, as these businesses tend to group together in buildings, anyway. If you plan on growing quickly, you could also negotiate a right of first refusal on any adjoining spaces, which gives you the first opportunity to expand into the space before it's leased to anyone else.

WHAT CAN BE NEGOTIATED?

Once the LOI is executed by the tenant and the land-lord, the lease negotiations will start. The good news is that almost everything in a commercial lease is nego-tiable. This can also be the bad news if there is a lot to discuss and agree on, as it can drag the process out quite a bit. The most complex leases can take months to finally execute.

However, it's Negotiating 101 that you won't go back on the deal points you already agreed to in the LOI. For example, once base rent has been signed off on by both parties in the LOI, it's considered bad manners to try to change it. Don't sign the LOI until it reflects an agreement on the key points, and this won't become an issue.

Before you start negotiating, identify your must-haves, which are your non-negotiables, and the things that might be nice to have but you're willing to sacrifice, if necessary. For example, a restaurant might absolutely require visi-bility, ease of access, customer parking, and a grease trap. The restaurant owner might also insist on rent abatement due to the build-out required and exclusivity. However, he might be willing to give up having a patio and a drive-through, which would really just be the cherry on top. Like the restaurant owner, know where you're going to stand strong and hold your ground, and know where you're willing to bend and give a little. This is the give-and-take that every good negotiation requires.

Remember, you aren't the only party involved in the transaction. The landlord will have a similar list of certain things he is unwilling to compromise on and the things he's willing to discuss. The majority of landlords want to work with you when they have vacant space that isn't bringing in any income. Look at them and treat them as a business partner. After all, they're investing in your business by taking the risk of putting you in their space. You'll stand a better chance of executing the lease if you're willing to participate in the give-and-take. When you compromise, the landlord will, too.

EXCLUSIVITY

Exclusivity is not always a non-negotiable, but it can be if it's important for the health of your business. For example, Kroger may insist on exclusivity in that they don't want another grocery store or bakery nearby. However, they may not care if a cupcake shop opens next door if it's small enough, even though they have a bakery that occasionally sells cupcakes.

If you have a very niche business, it's probably in your best interest if the same business isn't next door. For instance, it won't help the Mongolian barbecue restaurant to have another Mongolian barbecue in close proximity. Instead, the restaurant's must-have may be an exclusive use on Asian food in the shopping center where it's located. Subway would still be able to sell a teriyaki chicken sandwich nearby, because it isn't the restaurant's primary business, but a sushi restaurant couldn't open next door. Although fast food chains benefit from locating near other fast food restaurants, it's not the same if you are a local establishment or a specialty restaurant.

CO-TENANCY

When you are negotiating co-tenancy, it's very important to know who else is in the shopping center where you are planning to locate. If you're counting on traffic from the anchor tenants, such as Target or Publix, what happens if they leave?

Generally, small businesses will have a hard time negotiating a cancellation clause based on a large tenant vacating, but bigger stores do it routinely. For example, if Target closes in a shopping center, Stein Mart might be able to institute a rent reduction or a cancellation if the vacated spot is not replaced by a like tenant within a certain amount of time.

For smaller businesses, co-tenancy goes hand in hand

with exclusivity. If you're a nail salon, you will not want to be co-tenants with another nail salon. Instead, you'll require exclusivity. Or you may want to seek co-tenancy with a complementary tenant. A small ice-cream shop might want to be next to a sandwich shop that doesn't offer dessert (think TCBY and Subway), or a physical therapist might want to locate near a doctor's office. In these cases, the small business needs to consider the impact of the co-tenant vacating and protect themselves through adjustments in the lease.

CONTINGENCIES

There may be certain contingencies that the landlord is unable to compromise on, whether he wants to or not. For example, the landlord's lender may require in their loan agreement that the space cannot be leased for less than $17 per square foot. Otherwise, the landlord would be violating the loan agreement and the loan could be called. The landlord will not want to put his investment at risk, so his minimum rent will be no less than the requirement.

However, even the non-negotiable can be discussed and become part of a compromise. Shopping centers are valued based on the price per square foot they are achieving in rent, so the landlord is going to insist on the rent required by his loan agreement or more. However, the landlord might be willing to give a few months of free rent at the start of the lease to help you get up and running. This concession essentially brings your actual expense down significantly when calculated over the entire term of your lease.

Some other non-negotiable items might be liability insurance and common space rates, or the amount tenants share for hallways, restrooms, elevators, and so forth. However, when you are willing to be creative and discuss the possibilities, you may be able to get something in return for agreeing to those items.

BARTERING

When everything is negotiable, bartering becomes an option. Those involved in commercial real estate are the ultimate dealmakers. Although it's possible to have the seller or landlord throw in his Bentley to sweeten the deal (which I've seen happen), bartering is usually used in more traditional ways.

Bartering simply means that the parties to the transaction make a trade of products or services and there's no exchange of cash. It can be a win-win situation for the parties involved if the items traded are of equal value. For example, a landlord might reduce the rent for a tenant who runs a gym if the gym will provide services as an amenity for his building. If you have assets or skills that a landlord needs, you are in a good position to offer those services and structure a deal that makes sense for both of you.

THREE KEY POINTS

It's going to take some time to find the perfect commercial space for your business. Once you find it, you have to be willing to engage in the give-and-take that ultimately results in a lease.

EVERYTHING IS NEGOTIABLE

Negotiation is an art form. However, if you do your homework and are willing to compromise, you'll get what you want at the price you need.

IDENTIFY YOUR MUST-HAVES AND YOUR WOULD-BE-NICES

To win at the negotiating game, you not only have to know what you want, but you also have to have something to give. Before entering into any discussion about the lease, know exactly what you require and what you're willing to compromise on.

THE LOI IS NONBINDING

The LOI is not a lease or a contract. It's the prelude to the nitty-gritty of figuring out every point of the deal. Once you and the landlord agree to the LOI, you can move to the next step: negotiating the lease. Keep in mind that the landlord may be negotiating several different deals at the same time on the same property. Depending on the popularity of the area and the state of the market, you may want to submit LOIs on several properties to protect yourself. Use the process to your advantage and make the deal work on your terms, where possible.

5

SIGN THE LEASE

Congratulations! You've finalized the LOI and you're ready to move on to the lease. You're one step closer to calling the movers and printing new business cards.

Leases are typically drawn up on the landlord's standard form. There may be clauses in the landlord's lease that will require further negotiating, so you're back to some give-and-take.

Meet with your broker and attorney to discuss any changes or recommendations that they may have regarding the lease. While the primary deal points were settled on in the LOI, you still have the fine detail work to hammer out, such as who will pay for certain damages to the property.

AFTER THE LOI

Once you've received the lease from the landlord, read through it carefully. Make sure everything in the LOI is included. Rely on your team to help you understand and perfect the document in a way that works for both parties. Even if you're a great negotiator, you don't have any footing if you don't understand the terms or common pitfalls. Experienced brokers will be familiar with the standard clauses and can guide you through the technical aspects of the lease alongside your attorney.

Unlike the LOI, the lease is the guarantee that you can occupy the property. It's a legal document that should be reviewed by a real estate attorney. It's not necessary to have the attorney spend expensive hours on the lease, because your broker should be able to make some initial changes to protect your interests. Let your broker work on the lease, then send it to your attorney. Brokers are not attorneys and will give recommendations, not legal advice, but they do understand leases and can act as the first level of review.

THE PARTS OF YOUR LEASE

Just like the LOI, the lease will always include customary clauses. These clauses will be much more detailed and the main reason you will need your broker and attorney involved at the very beginning. Depending on the sophistication of your landlord, your lease will likely include the following:

1. Notice addresses: These are the official addresses where the parties receive mail.
2. Property description: Much more than an address, this is the legal description of the property.
3. Security deposit: What is it securing? When is it refundable? Can it be applied toward your rent?
4. Rent adjustments: How much will your rent increase monthly? Annually?
5. Use of premises: Detailed discussion of how you are allowed to use the premises. The purpose of this clause is to protect other tenants from disruptive activities.
6. Common area operating expenses: What will you have to pay for common areas? What will the landlord maintain, and what is your responsibility?
7. Defaults by either party: This clause defines what constitutes default (i.e., late rent payment by tenant, failure to maintain the building by landlord) and the available remedies.
8. Building access: Is there twenty-four-hour access to the building? Or is the HVAC turned off at 7:00 p.m.?
9. Holdover at the end of the lease: The typical fee for staying in the space after the lease term ends is 150 percent of current rent.

10. Insurance, indemnification, and liability: How much insurance is required by each party? Which party is responsible if someone is injured on the property?
11. Lawsuit guidelines: This clause sets forth choice of law and venue in case of a lawsuit and whether arbitration is required.

Although you'll typically see all of these items discussed in a lease, no two leases are the same. Landlords often have expensive attorneys craft their own leases, so it's not surprising that they will be somewhat skewed in the drafter's favor. This doesn't mean the lease can't be changed or negotiated. It just means that you need to have your broker and attorney representing you at all times. Remember, your lease will be one of your business's biggest expense items, and you cannot take this process lightly.

THE REAL ESTATE ATTORNEY

Although you may be tempted to accept the lease without a legal review, using an attorney is highly recommended. You use legal counsel in many areas of your business, and real estate should be no different. Expert guidance is necessary because business owners are generally unaware of the pitfalls hidden in lease negotiations. Landlords do this for a living and still hire professionals to represent them—don't get taken advantage of.

Just like commercial real estate brokers versus residential agents, all attorneys are not created equal. Even if you already have a business attorney, you need to find someone who specializes in real estate law. Look for an attorney who is negotiating leases and reviewing contracts on a regular basis. They know what to be looking for and will approach your deal with the mindset of making it work for you. Your broker can recommend a good real estate attorney, if you don't know where to look.

Let your broker review the lease first and add comments before sending to your attorney. Once your attorney receives the lease, he should be able to complete his review within three to five days, depending on the length of the lease and his own workload. The benefits of hiring an attorney, regardless of their hourly or set rate, far outweigh the costs when you consider the fact that they could save you tens of thousands of dollars by changing one sentence. It pays to have experts working for you who know how to get the job done.

TIPS TO REMEMBER

Nothing is standard in lease negotiation. The landlord is an expert at knowing what's in his best interest, and there are some things you should keep in mind to protect yours.

FREE RENT

Landlords do give free rent, but you have to ask for it. There are reasons that justify free rent, and landlords understand them. For example, you may not want to start paying rent until you are moved in and customers are coming through the doors. Or you may want two months of free rent to complete your build-out. It's not unusual for a landlord to compromise and give you the time you need before you are charged rent.

If the landlord does agree to waive your rent payment, pay attention to when the free rent countdown starts. Does it start at the signing of the lease or when you open for business? If you are doing a build-out, does it start once you have a construction permit or before? These are important considerations that can be leveraged to your advantage.

READ YOUR LEASE

You must read your lease, because the future of your business depends on it. I know it's incredibly boring and uninteresting to you, but it's a binding contract. If you don't understand your responsibilities under the lease, you're much more likely to violate the terms and get evicted or sued.

Absent an amendment, which both parties must agree

on, the lease is unchangeable once the ink is dry. There's no guarantee that your landlord will agree to an amendment, however, so you need to get it right the first time. Read your lease thoroughly and understand your legal obligations before moving forward. Use your broker and attorney to clarify terms and answer questions.

CONSTRUCTION DOCUMENTS

If you are doing a build-out, construction documents become very important. You will need a site plan and as-builts to know the details of the mechanical and electrical systems and so forth. Reference these in your lease and have the landlord provide them within a certain time period. This will help you avoid expensive delays or extra cost in having a third party re-create the documents.

LANDLORD AND TENANT RESPONSIBILITIES

In most leases, it's standard that the landlord maintains the exterior (structural aspects) of the building and the tenant maintains the interior. This may change, however, if it's a single-tenant building. Make sure you know what is expected of you and what your landlord is agreeing to take care of.

Always get the plumbing, electrical, and HVAC inspected

before you sign a lease. You want to know exactly what you are inheriting. If your plumbing is 50 percent blocked when you sign the lease, you just accepted a faulty system, and you'll have to pay for it to be fixed. If the HVAC is twelve years old, you need to know that it's a risk. Be careful that the lease doesn't give you full responsibility for the HVAC, especially if it's an older system.

One way to negotiate the responsibility for the HVAC is to put a cap on the fees. Landlords may be willing to compromise if you sign a maintenance contract and agree to pay for minor repairs. Protect yourself by capping the amount you are willing to pay per year to $1,000 annually, or whatever is reasonable in the situation.

RESTRICTIONS

Restrictions in a lease refer to the things that you are *not* allowed to do. If you do them, you will be in violation of the lease and may have to pay a penalty, or you might be evicted. A common violation occurs in the context of other tenant's exclusivities. For example, a nail salon may have an exclusivity when it comes to offering manicures in the building. If the hair salon next door starts doing nails, they would be in violation of the lease, and the nail salon tenant could seek remedies. The best way to avoid the issue is to know your lease and abide by its terms.

ADDITIONAL RESOURCES

Even though you have an attorney and a broker, it never
hurts to educate yourself about commercial real estate.
For more information about commercial real estate leases
and negotiation, these books will be helpful:

- *Negotiating Commercial Real Estate Leases*, Martin I.
  Zankel.
- *The Art of Commercial Real Estate Leasing: How to Lease
  a Commercial Building and Keep It Leased*, R. Craig
  Coppola. This book will give you insight into the land-
  lord's point of view.
- *The Leasing Process: Landlord and Tenant Perspectives*,
  Richard F. Muhlebach and Alan A. Alexander.

FATAL MISTAKES TO AVOID WHEN LEASING COMMERCIAL SPACE

Mistake 1: Underestimating the time it takes to find and lease a new space.

Is your current lease term coming to an end? Or are you thinking of opening a new business? Depending on how active your market is and what industry you're in, finding a new location could take anywhere from one week to several months or even years. Remember that your time line doesn't end once you've set your eyes on a site. You still have to negotiate the lease and give yourself additional time for tenant improvements (build-outs).

Solution: Be proactive and allot enough time to find a new space, negotiate a deal, and complete any additions/alterations. I highly recommend at least three months' lead time, which should be enough for most businesses. However, I have been involved in deals that took four-plus months to negotiate terms and finalize construction. It's better to play it safe. Start reviewing your options six to twelve months out and have a thorough, concise strategy for reentering the leasing market. Take your time so you can get the right deal for your company; don't get caught in a situation where you have to make a decision too fast.

Mistake 2: Not negotiating the lease.

Landlords are very aware of how to indemnify and protect themselves in the lease. They have spent a lot of time and money crafting the contract to protect their best interests, not yours. Negotiating a lease won't seem like second nature to you (like it is for landlords) unless you've done it before, so educate yourself and know how to approach the situation.

Solution: Whether you're looking for retail, office, or industrial space, every lease is negotiable. Each minute detail in a commercial lease, from length of term to how much of the construction the landlord will provide, can be removed, altered, amended, or added. An empty space can be very expensive for a landlord, so they are typically willing to give more concessions on a longer lease to avoid dealing with such vacancy again in the near future. Want a kitchenette installed? Need a few walls removed? What about street signage and brand visibility? Ask for it.

Mistake 3: Going it alone.

Running your business is already difficult enough without throwing in market research, site selection, lease negotiations, and everything else commercial real estate can throw at you. The landlord's business is commercial real estate, which gives him a serious edge during negotiations. You wouldn't go to trial without a lawyer, right? The same applies to commercial real estate.

Solution: Put together an all-star team that has fiduciary responsibility to you. I recommend a tenant broker (which is at no cost to you; the landlord typically pays their fees), a real estate lawyer, and a CPA. Tenant brokers should know of deals that are off-market, which can lead to negotiating a better deal. These brokers deal with commercial leasing every day. Many have taken advanced classes on contract negotiation and know the little details that could make or break your business. After the broker has helped you determine the right location and made his recommendations of lease additions or alterations, a lawyer will scour the text to make sure you are protected legally. CPAs will help you run the numbers and determine what your budget should be, which will be site specific. Remember that the right location can make your revenue skyrocket.

THREE KEY POINTS

Once you have agreed to the details of the deal, they will be memorialized in a legal contract. The negotiating process for a commercial lease can be grueling, but getting it right is worth the trouble. A client once noted that "a lot of little nuances in the lease can make the difference in the success of your business." He wasn't being overdramatic. With the right guidance, your lease will protect you in times of growth, as well as in times that aren't so great.

Let's put it this way: if your base rent is $4,000 per month on a five-year term, you will be investing $240,000 on your location, not including utilities or any additional expenses. That's the cost of a single-family home. Take your representation seriously and make sure that those "little nuances" don't come back to haunt you.

ALWAYS READ YOUR LEASE

It can't be emphasized enough that you should always read your lease, even when you have guidance from an attorney and broker. It's common sense that you need to understand your obligations before you sign on the dotted line. A bad lease can make you shut your doors, but a good one will be a sword and shield to protect you and help you prosper.

COMPARE THE LEASE TO THE LOI

You've already negotiated and agreed to most of the major deal points in the LOI. Double-check your lease and make sure these points are reflected exactly as previously established. It's bad form to renegotiate the points that were already settled, but it never hurts to compare the two documents to ensure all negotiated points made it into the final contract.

USE YOUR ATTORNEY

Real estate attorneys are specialists in leases and contracts. They deal in commercial real estate issues every day and know what to look for and how to protect you. Let them do their job, and don't hesitate to call on them to help you understand what you're signing.

6

BUILD-OUTS

It's very common for commercial spaces to require some design work before they're ready for occupancy. Some spaces will be fully renovated, but others will need you to implement your own design and renovations. Second-generation spaces usually require updating at the very least, or a total makeover in the worst of cases.

The build-out is the work that will be done to make the property ready for your business. It can be as big and impressive as you like, and the changes can add personality, as well as functionality, to your business. On the other hand, a build-out may not be necessary if the space is laid out efficiently. You may take a utilitarian approach and simply freshen up the space with new paint and carpet.

As you view potential spaces, it's a good idea to know your design requirements in as much detail as possible in order to judge how much build-out is necessary. Think about the number of offices you need and what kind of open space should be included. Decide on additional rooms or areas that you must have. Will there be a kitchen? A waiting room? Do you need closets or storage areas?

As you compare properties, the build-out will be part of your cost-benefit analysis. For example, you may find the perfect location, but the new space isn't functional. You'll have to decide if it makes sense to lease in that area and spend the money and time on the build-out, or if it's wiser to go somewhere else.

Market conditions play a big role in whether you can find exactly what you need without the expense of a build-out. If there's a lot of product available in a down market, you may strike property gold without too much trouble. However, when demand is high, spaces are leased very quickly and what you need may not be available. In a hot market, you may have to modify the space or settle for a property that's not ideal.

PAYING FOR THE BUILD-OUT

The catchphrase of the negotiation stage can be applied

to the build-out as well: everything is negotiable. All modifications to the property will be discussed and become a part of the lease before any changes are made. The landlord may agree to cover the cost, the tenant might take on the responsibility, or the cost of the build-out may be shared.

Landlords know that their property will not work for every business, and they understand that tenants don't want to pay for improvements to spaces they don't own. For these reasons, the landlord may be willing to pay for all of the changes with a turnkey build-out. On the flipside, if your use is very specific to your business or industry, the landlord may not be as willing to help you financially on the build-out, because they'll likely have to fully renovate the space for the following tenant.

Although it saves money and is an easy way to get the space ready for move-in, the turnkey build-out can have drawbacks. The landlord may be tempted to use cheaper materials or hire cheaper labor that results in shoddy work. If this is a concern, address it in the negotiations and include it in your contract by specifying the level of quality, or the general contractor that must be used. Generally, this isn't a big concern because the alterations are reflections on the property, and the landlord will not want to decrease the value of his investment.

If you'd rather have control over the process, you might choose to pay for the build-out yourself. Even in this case, the alterations to the space are mutually agreed upon. The difference is that you're completely in charge of the construction. You hire the architect or contractor, and you are responsible for everything from the placement of electrical outlets to construction of the walls. In this instance, you'll negotiate for a tenant improvement (TI) allowance from the landlord to cover the costs of the build-out. TI is often referred to in dollars per square foot. For example, if your space is two thousand square feet and your landlord has offered to give you $20 per square foot for a TI allowance, that is $40,000 that may be applied toward the construction of your space.

It's important to keep track of all of your expenses because you will need to pay for any build-out costs above and beyond that original amount. Landlords will typically reimburse the TI allowance to the tenant following the completion of the build-out upon receipt of all lien waivers and construction bills.

The build-out negotiations may result in the cost being shared between the parties. For example, office buildings typically offer new paint and carpet when a tenant moves in. The choices may be limited to standard finishes, or the tenant may be given a specific budget and he can choose anything within the amount provided. The tenant may decide he wants custom finishes and would pay for those upgrades himself.

The build-out doesn't have to be a huge expense. Weigh your options and figure out what makes the most sense for you. For example, a business owner who is under a huge time crunch may be willing to waive the new paint and carpet offered by his landlord because it would delay his move. Instead, the tenant could negotiate a rent abatement at the level of the build-out that the landlord was originally willing to cover. Compromises like this are commonplace in commercial real estate when you simply *ask*.

BUILDING STANDARDS

Building standards can't be overlooked during the build-out because the look of your space needs to match your brand. For example, an architecture firm that wanted their originality and design acumen to be reflected in their offices was unimpressed with the standard finishes offered by their landlord. The parties negotiated a satisfactory result for all. The landlord paid for $80,000 of the $100,000 custom build-out, and the firm picked up the rest of the tab. The firm got the look they wanted for a fraction of the cost, the building benefited from the upgrades, and both parties were amenable to the split in fees.

Every business will not demand such remarkable build-outs, but you should consider the impression you want to make on your clients. Clearly, for a design and architecture firm, they wanted to display their capability to any potential client who walked through the door. Cutting corners on design or construction doesn't make sense when you have only one chance to make a good impression.

You can also use your build-out to show off the personality of your business. When a business chooses to show its clientele who they are and what they do, it attracts the business they want.

If customers will never see your office, you may not need the "wow" factor. However, if you entertain high-end customers or provide a luxury product or service, you may have to increase your spend on the front end so the space fits your business. A warehouse doesn't need anything but the basics, but a spa should embody the luxury and extravagance that its clients expect.

Dentists' offices are among the most expensive to build-out, tipping the scales at over $120 per square foot. Think about it: If you're going to sit in a chair and let someone put a drill in your mouth, you want to be in competent, professional hands. The dentist's office that hasn't been updated since the 1980s, with worn carpets and chipped paint on the walls, won't do the job and will scare off customers.

MILLENNIALS AND OFFICE DESIGN

The custom quality of your build-out is not only a reflection of your brand to the outside world, but it may also be important to your current and future employees. Studies show that the way you design your space impacts the creativity and productivity of the people working for you. Understanding what the surroundings say about your business will help you attract the level of talent you require.

For example, millennials (people born between the 1980s and 2000) are one of the largest generations in history, and they are moving into their prime employment years. By 2025, millennials will make up more than 75 percent of the workforce. They are poised to revolutionize the way we work.

If you want to attract millennials to your business, your work environment should reflect the kind of place they want to be in. Google is among those leading the charge in this area. They are the pinnacle of millennial "cool" with coffee shops, collaboration rooms, and bikes for getting to other buildings. They even call their compound a "campus." Google knows what their millennial employees want, and they are willing to provide it in order to attract the best. Their office design features living room-type spaces with sofas and beanbags, as well as open work areas and long tables instead of private offices, so employees can work side by side with their colleagues. It's much different than the world of their parents, who treasured the privacy and cachet of the large corner office. By creating this environment, Google is able to keep employees on campus longer, working at higher levels of creativity.

Your office design can be used to tell the world what kind of business you are, but it's making a statement to your employees as well. The build-out is an opportunity to speak volumes. So what is it that you want to say?

COMPLETING THE BUILD-OUT

Even if you were a bricklayer in high school and are now a master at putting together IKEA cabinets, avoid the temptation to do the build-out yourself. Hire a general contractor and use your experience for oversight on the job. Having a professional in charge will give you peace of mind, and landlords generally require that a licensed professional do the work.

In fact, your choice of commercial contractor may be decided by the building owner, who will be concerned about the quality of work performed on their property. Landlords like to know who is doing the work that will affect their investment and who will be working inside the rented space that may house other businesses. They may have a required contractor for you to use, or they may want to inspect the license of the contractor you hire.

Depending on the size and style of your business, you might benefit from hiring an architect, interior designer, or space planner. An architect is necessary if you are doing any structural or specialized work that requires permits. The city will want to see your construction plans stamped by an architect before you're able to move forward.

Even if you don't need to go as far as hiring an architect, an interior designer or space planner can help you design and lay out your space in the most effective and efficient ways. Paying an expert now may directly impact your bottom line down the road. For example, a dental office that put four dental chairs in a space might have fit six with advice from an expert space planner. That office could have serviced two additional clients every hour.

Professionals are instrumental in getting the most out of your space, but they can also help with color and furniture choice. These details create an ambience that can impact your corporate culture and how your employees interact.

CHOOSING A CONTRACTOR

Make sure you hire a commercial contractor, not the residential contractor who builds homes in your neighborhood. A commercial build-out is not a residential renovation. I'm sure you've noticed a recurring theme throughout this book: hire the professionals who specialize in the commercial real estate field. It's very different from other specializations within each industry, and you need the most competent team on your side.

In a public space, you have to pay attention to commercial building codes, which are very different from residential requirements. Even the best residential contractor may not be familiar with ADA requirements or differences in fire codes.

Residential contractors may also be unfamiliar with commercial grade materials. Residential grade carpet will not stand up to the wear and tear of having twenty people walking on it every day. Two thousand square feet of carpet in an office space is not the equivalent of two-thousand square feet of carpet in your home.

Good contractors can save you time and money, but bad ones can be disastrous. Picking the right contractor doesn't have to be difficult, but it does require some careful thought. It's a big decision that will have a big impact on your business.

The best contractor is not always the cheapest one, and spending less shouldn't be your deciding factor. It would be wise to get three bids and compare the offers. If one is very high and one is very low, you may want to go with the one in the middle. There are reasons the other two were at the far ends of the spectrum. However, if all three are approximately the same cost for the same scope of work, the cheaper alternative could be a good bet.

The way you and your contractor get along during the initial bid process should play a significant role in determining whom you should hire. If you don't get along in the walk-through, you won't get along throughout construction.

Ask for references and look for reviews of potential contractors online. Contracting is different from most industries because their work is literally on view for all to see. The person who commissioned the work can determine very quickly if the contractor did a good job or a terrible one, and they usually don't mind sharing that information.

If the price is right and the reviews are good, the next step is to interview the contractor. You have to be able to develop a rapport and be comfortable talking to him. Evaluate his communication style and how quickly he responds to you when you call. If he's too difficult to get in touch with or too slow to respond, he may not be the best fit.

Your general contractor is your connection to all of the work getting done. He may know how to do all of it, but he won't be doing all of the work himself. Instead, he'll hire subcontractors while he orchestrates the timing.

Even if you have a friend who could do some of the construction, it's best to let the GC hire his own crew. Because he's ultimately responsible for the subcontractor's work, he's not going to hire anyone unless he's familiar with their skill and work ethic. You don't want to be the one having to follow up with a subcontractor to get their work done simply because you wanted to use that sub. It's not fun, and it never works out in the way you'd like it to.

Stories about untrustworthy subcontractors are prevalent in the real estate market. For example, a tenant who insisted that the GC hire his friend for flooring ended up paying the price. The GC took a chance and hired the friend instead of using the subcontractor he usually used. He didn't stay on schedule and did a terrible job. When the subcontractor was called back in to clean up excess glue on the floor, he flushed the cleanup rags down the toilet in protest, flooding the floors. Not only did the tenant have to pay to redo the floors due to the damage, but he also had to pay to fix the plumbing. Lesson learned—don't interfere.

PLAN EVERYTHING

Although it may be a tedious process, plan everything in your space down to the tiniest detail *before* you start construction or renovation. Think about the layout, but also consider the light fixtures, the outlet placement, and even the direction the doors will swing as they open and close.

Without planning, you could end up with no overhead

lights or only one outlet per room. Depending on the type of business, this could be very expensive to go back and retrofit. A good commercial contractor knows what to look for and can help with your decision making if necessary. They will also follow your instructions to the letter, so be clear and detailed.

TIMING

The amount of time needed to complete a build-out is dependent on the scope of work and the type of business that is relocating. In a retail or office space, the typical build-out should take thirty to ninety days. Unfortunately, build-outs are rarely typical. If you have to tear out walls, add plumbing, or rearrange the electrical system, ninety days may not be long enough. You never know what you'll find when you start demolition.

A restaurant build-out also requires more time. Restaurants have more time-consuming additions such as water lines, hood vents, and grease traps. It's more complicated and may take up to five or six months. Preparation will help immensely here, as you can't afford to have any delays.

Special ordering materials to satisfy your design preferences will extend your time line as well. It's not uncommon for carpet typical of an office building to be several weeks on backorder or for cabinets to take months. But if you keep it simple and freshen the space with only standard carpet and paint, you'll be moving in a short few weeks.

Try to closely approximate the time it will take before you open for business. It's important for financial planning but will also be helpful during lease negotiations. Use your team and rely on your broker to help you develop an accurate time line. They've done it before, and their frame of reference may be greater than your own.

THREE KEY POINTS

The build-out can be the most important step in the process of finding and leasing a new home for your business. Your customers will be forming opinions of your business based on what your space looks like and how it functions. Make the most of the opportunity.

CONSIDER WORKING WITH A SPACE PLANNER

Space planners understand how people operate within a space. They can make suggestions to improve the flow and functionality of the layout.

HIRE A COMMERCIAL CONTRACTOR

Even if you think you can do it yourself, hiring a licensed commercial contractor will save money and time on your project. This is another case of hiring the right person for the job and letting them do what they do best. Commercial contractors are in the industry, will build according to commercial codes, and have a roster of subcontractors with a reputation for good work.

KEEP YOUR IMAGE IN MIND

The look of your new space is a direct reflection of your business. It's an opportunity to connect with customers and satisfy your staff. Color and design can be used as a tool to support your brand and bring the perfect employees to your door.

CONCLUSION

OPEN FOR BUSINESS

It's been quite the journey to reach this point. You found the perfect space, negotiated your lease, completed the build-out, and now you're ready to put the "Open for Business" sign on the door. It's an exciting milestone, but it's important to refer to your lease throughout its term and fully understand your continuing responsibilities and obligations.

AFTER THE LEASE

Your lease is a legal document. When you signed it, you committed to doing, or not doing, certain things. You can't put your lease in a desk drawer and forget about it.

Instead, work with your broker to make sure you know what needs to be done to avoid default. You can always call your broker if you ever have any questions throughout the lease term.

THE LEASE CHEAT SHEET

Your biggest responsibility is to pay your rent and pay it on time. Your lease includes the due date and the penalties for missing it. Put it on your calendar or do whatever you need to do to satisfy the landlord's requirements.

Lean on your broker or attorney to create a "lease cheat sheet." Instead of digging through a thirty-page document to find pertinent information, your cheat sheet is an outline of things you need to pay special attention to, such as specific dates, responsibilities, and the landlord's notice address. Anything that you might need to refer to during your lease term can be added to help you stay on track.

The purpose of the landlord's notice address is to make sure you have an official address to use for contacting your landlord. This is especially important as you get close to the end of your lease term. Your lease will specify the notice required or what you need to do if you want to renegotiate and extend the term. Holdover fees add up quickly at 150 or 200 percent of your rent, and if you hold over when the landlord has already found a new tenant, you may have to pay damages as well.

Six months before your lease expires, evaluate your needs. Do you still like the area? Have you outgrown the space? How is your relationship with your landlord?

Your landlord will want to know your plans, and you need to decide if you want to renegotiate or if you want to look for a new space. Time is of the essence if you want to move, especially if a build-out is needed.

Call your broker for assistance and information about the market. Good brokers are in it for the long haul and will be happy to help you with new negotiations or finding another potential property.

MONTHLY ACCOUNTING

If the landlord negotiated percentage rent, pay close attention to your bookkeeping. Percentage rent is most often seen in shopping mall leases, but you can find them anywhere in retail. Typically, the tenant is required to pay a percentage of gross revenue, or sales above some predetermined revenue goal, often your break-even point. In this case, you'll have to provide a monthly accounting to your landlord to show what you owe for the month.

The landlord will need to know your sales so they know what to collect.

SAVING MONEY

Common area expenses are building expenses that are split among the tenants. Typically, you will pay your pro rata share. If you occupy 10 percent of the building, you will be charged 10 percent of the common area expenses, which might include things such as snow removal, landscaping, janitorial services, and more.

Negotiate audit rights with the landlord regarding common area expenses to make sure you aren't being overcharged. For example, if your landlord rents space next to your business to a water park, it wouldn't be fair to charge you 50 percent of the water bill. Similarly, if there is very little grass in your office park, $10,000 for mowing expenses over the year is overreaching.

EXPANSION

The best way to handle potential growth of your business is to address it during lease negotiations. If you think you are going to be expanding quickly, ask the landlord for a right of first refusal on other spaces in the building. They may not be willing to give you official rights, but if they know you want the spot, they'll notify you prior to leasing it to anyone else.

Pay attention to lease restrictions if you are contemplating growth or adding a product line. You may not be allowed to stay where you are if you add a service or item that is in direct competition with another tenant. Check your lease, follow the terms, and talk to your broker or landlord before doing anything that might be a violation.

LOOKING AHEAD

You landed in the perfect place for your business to grow. For the next five years, or whatever the term of your lease may be, you will be tending to your business and following the terms of your lease. The time will eventually come when you are ready to make another move.

Leasing commercial real estate can be a difficult process. Moving your business is stressful. However, if you plan ahead, and plan with the right people, you will avoid most of the common pitfalls.

Stay in touch with your broker and don't go it alone. Use his knowledge of the market and expertise in the industry to help you throughout your term in the current location. Treat your broker as your own in-house real estate department. Let him advise you as you get closer to making a change or renegotiating to stay right where you are.

Remember everything you've learned about the process so far. Continue to learn as you go, and the next time around will be easier. Until then, do what all great leaders do: surround yourself with a specialized team of experts that will allow you to focus on the reason you embarked on this path to begin with—your business.

Leasing commercial real estate is a big step. It's one of the largest investments you can make as a business owner. However, if you follow the steps in this book, you can protect that investment and feel confident as you take your business to new heights.

For further information and tools, please visit my website at www.tylercauble.com/leasing-tips.

GLOSSARY

In any business endeavor, it's helpful when all of the parties "speak the same language," or assign the same meanings to words. Commercial real estate is no different. The following are terms used in commercial real estate and throughout this book. Being familiar with them will help you understand your deal and make you a smarter negotiator.

Actual Year Built: The year of construction.

Additional Description: Additional information on a property notice that describes the property.

Additional Rent: Charges to a tenant that are not included in the usable square footage or other rent costs, such as after-hours services, HVAC, common area maintenance (CAM) fees, and so on.

Add-On Factor: The ratio of rentable to usable square feet. Also known as the load factor.

Adjusted Basis: The original cost basis of a property plus capital improvement, less total accumulated cost recovery deductions and partial sales taken during the holding period.

Amortization: The repayment of loan principal through equal payments of both principal and interest over a designated period of time.

Assessment: The assessed value of the property used to determine value for tax purposes. The local tax rate is applied to this number to determine the amount of property taxes due.

Assessment Percentage: The percentage applied to the final appraisal to determine the assessment. Assessment percentages are based on property classification and are set by state law.

Aux Base Square Feet: The total number of square feet in areas of the building auxiliary to the base area, such as porches, garages, and so forth.

Balloon Payment: The final payment of the balance due on a partially amortized loan.

Base Area Square Feet: The total number of square feet in the main area of the building.

Base Rent: Minimum rent due under the terms of a lease. Additional rent may be required based on other factors.

Bldgs (or #bldgs): A count of the number of major improvements (i.e., buildings) on a parcel.

Building #: A number identifying a building on a parcel that is useful when there are multiple buildings on the parcel.

Building Value: The appraised value of the building.

Build-Out: Work required to make a property ready for its intended purpose.

Commercial Industrial Space: Property used for industrial purposes such as manufacturing, research and development parks, factory-office or factory-warehouse multiuse property, and industrial parks.

Common Area Maintenance (CAM): The CAM charge is

additional rent, charged on top of base rent, and is mainly composed of maintenance fees for work performed on the common area of a property.

Common Area Maintenance Cap (CAM Cap): The maximum amount the tenant pays for his share of common area maintenance costs.

Capital Gain: Taxable income derived from the sale of a capital asset. It is equal to the sales price less the cost of sale, adjusted basis, suspended losses, excess cost recovery, and recapture of straight-line cost recovery.

Capitalization Rate (Cap Rate): A cap rate is the ratio of net operating income (NOI) to the property asset value. If a property is listed at $500,000.00 with an NOI of $75,000.00, the cap rate would be 15 percent (75,000.00/500,000.00 = 0.15).

Cash Flow: The net cash received in any period, taking into account net operating income, debt service, capital expenses, loan proceeds, sale revenues, and any other sources and uses of cash.

Cash-on-Cash Return: A return measure that is calculated as cash flow before taxes divided by the initial equity investment.

Commercial Real Estate: Any multifamily residential, office, industrial, or retail property that can be bought or sold in a real estate market.

Common Area: Areas of the site available to all tenants for use on a nonexclusive basis, such as hallways, parking lots, roofs, and so forth.

Condition: The observed state of repair of a building upon its last inspection.

Contract Rent: The total rental obligation as specified in a lease. Also known as base rent.

Cost of Occupancy: The cost of occupying and maintaining a space.

Co-tenancy: The situation when more than one business shares a leased space. A co-tenancy clause in a commercial lease allows for a reduction in rent if other key tenants leave.

DBA: Doing Business As. A pseudonym used by a company to perform its business that differs from the registered legal name of the business.

Demographics: Characteristics of human populations as

defined by population size and density of regions, population growth rates, migration, vital statistics, and their effect on socioeconomic conditions.

Depreciation: The loss of utility and value of a property over time. Depreciation may be used as a tax write-off for a designated number of years.

Due Diligence: The process of examining a property and related documents, and the procedures conducted by or for the potential lender or purchaser to reduce risk.

Economic Characteristics: Aspects of the workforce, including production and employment activities.

Economic Obsolescence: An incurable loss of value or depreciation of a property due to unfavorable conditions external to the property, such as the local economy, loss of material or labor sources, new legislation, and so forth.

Effective Rent: An amount after the base rent has been adjusted for concessions, allowances, and costs.

Electrical: All of the wiring for the distribution of electricity, along with the fixtures and outlets.

Environmental Hazards: Any physical or natural condition or event that poses a risk to humans.

Environmental Impacts: Possible adverse environmental effects caused by an activity or specific land use or by the release of a substance into the environment.

Exclusivity: A clause in a commercial lease that acts as a protection for the tenant. It prohibits the landlord from leasing space to others that would engage in the same line of business as the original tenant.

Expense Stop: The maximum amount a landlord will pay for certain operating expenses.

Exterior Wall: The portion of a building enclosing the entire building area consisting of all parts of the structural system including framing and cover material.

Feasibility Analysis: The process of evaluating a proposed project to determine if it will meet the objectives set forth by the parties involved (i.e., owners, investors, developers, lessees).

Fixed Costs: Costs that do not change with a building's occupancy rate. They include property taxes, insurance, and some forms of building maintenance.

Fixed Lease: A lease in which the rental amount will not change for the duration of the term.

Flex Space: Space that is flexible in terms of its use, such as a building with four thousand square feet of office space and two thousand square feet of warehouse.

Floor Finish: The material that overlays the slab or subfloor.

Floor System: The part of a building immediately above the foundation and below the floor finish.

Foundation: The part of the building beneath the floor system.

Free Rent: See *Rent Concession*.

Full-Service Gross (FSG): In an FSG lease, the landlord is responsible for paying the taxes, maintenance, insurance, and utilities for the premises.

Full-Service Lease: A lease structure under which the tenant pays rent that is all inclusive. The landlord covers all other occupancy expenses such as taxes and maintenance.

Generic Space: Commercial space that can be used for a variety of purposes.

Government Incentive: Concession provided by local or regional government to attract business or investment dollars to an area to promote economic growth.

Gross Area: The total square footage of a building or floor.

Gross Lease: A type of commercial lease that requires the landlord pay all "usual costs" associated with owning and maintaining a rented space such as utilities, water and sewer, repairs, insurance, and taxes.

Gross Rent Multiplier (GRM): A tool investors use to calculate the ratio of the price of a real estate investment to its annual rental income after expenses. The GRM is used to determine the number of years it will take for a property to pay for itself in gross received rent.

Ground Lease: A lease of the land only, typically for an extended period so that a developer or tenant may construct a building.

Heating, Ventilation, and Air Conditioning (HVAC): The source of heating and cooling a building and the system for distributing it throughout a building.

Highest and Best Use: The reasonably probable and legal use of vacant land or an improved property that is physically possible, appropriately supported, financially feasible, and that results in the highest value.

Holdover Tenant: A tenant who stays on the premises after the expiration of the original lease term.

Intangible Characteristics: Property attributes that are not directly measurable or quantifiable.

Interior Finish: The main finish on the inside partition walls.

Inventory: The supply of a given commodity.

Kickout: A lease clause that allows a tenant or landlord to cancel the lease after a certain time has passed or certain conditions have or have not been met.

Labor Pool: The group of workers that make up the local labor force.

Landlord: A person or business that leases land, buildings, or residential space to a tenant.

Landlord-Paid Tenant Improvements (LPTI): The total cost of improvements paid by the landlord netted against any tenant contributions.

Lease: A legally binding document detailing the terms of your real estate agreement.

Lease Buyout: The process of extinguishing a tenant's remaining lease obligations and rights under an existing lease.

Leasehold Estate: Ownership by a tenant of a temporary right to occupy and use a property for the duration of a lease in exchange for rent.

Leasing: A means of obtaining the use of a property for a specified term without ownership.

Lessee: Another term for a tenant.

Lessor: Another term for a landlord.

Letter of Intent (LOI): A document outlining one or more agreements between two or more parties before the agreements are finalized by a contract. It is typically nonbinding.

Load Factor: A way of calculating total monthly rent costs that combines usable square feet and a percentage of square feet of the common areas.

Marketability: The attractiveness of a property in terms of how quickly it will sell or lease.

Market Analysis: The process of examining a market in terms of value and volume to determine commercial feasibility or suitability of various locations for a given purpose.

Market Area: A geographical area in which supply and demand operate to influence industrial and commercial activities.

Market Data: Information collected for a given market or market area.

Market Data Approach: Determining a property's value by analyzing recent sales or rental prices of comparable properties.

Market Gap: The demand for space minus the supply of space for a given type of commercial property in a certain market.

Market Pricing: The pricing of rental rates as determined by the factors of influence in a market.

Market Value: The most probable price that a property

would bring in a competitive and open market under fair sale conditions.

Metropolitan Statistical Area (MSA): The area in and around a major city.

Moving Allowance: A determined amount that a landlord or owner will pay to cover a tenant's moving expenses.

Multiple-Use Office Space: Generic office space that can be used for a variety of purposes.

Net Lease: A lease in which the tenant pays all operating expenses in addition to rent (i.e., taxes, insurance, maintenance).

Net Operating Income: The potential rental income plus other income, less vacancy, credit losses, and operating expenses.

Occupancy Cost: The actual dollars paid out by a tenant to occupy a space.

Operating Expenses: Cash outlays necessary to operate and maintain a property (i.e., taxes, insurance, maintenance, management, utilities, legal, accounting).

Operating expenses do not include capital expenditures, debt service, or cost recovery.

Option: A clause in a commercial lease that allows the tenant to renew the lease for a certain time if certain conditions are met.

Pass-Throughs: Operating expenses for the premises that are passed on to the tenant by the landlord.

Percentage Lease: Lease requiring the tenant pay a base rent plus a percentage based on monthly sales volumes.

Potential Rental Income: The total rental income for a property if it were 100 percent occupied and rented at commercial rates.

Property Type: The classification of commercial real estate based on its primary use as retail, industrial, office, and multifamily residential.

Rate of Return: The percentage return on each dollar invested. Also known as yield.

Real Estate Cycles: The regularly repeating sequence of events reflected in demographic, economic, and emotional factors that affect supply and demand for property.

Rent Concession: A period of free rent given to the tenant by the lessor.

Rent Escalators: Items specified in a lease such as base rent, operating expenses, and taxes that may increase by predetermined amounts at stated intervals or by a constant annual percentage.

Replacement Cost: The estimated cost to construct, at current prices, a building equivalent to the building at issue.

Sandwich Lease: See *Sublease*.

Second-Generation Space: Property that has been occupied and improved by a previous tenant.

Site Analysis: The evaluation of a specific site regarding its ability to satisfy a given use or objective.

Site Selection: The process of determining the best site for a specific use.

Square Feet: The unit used to measure the floor area of a space. For example, if a space is 20 feet wide and 60 feet deep, it would be 1,200 square feet (20' x 60').

Step-Up Lease: A lease in which the rental amount paid by

the lessee increases by a preset rate or set dollar amount at predetermined intervals. A step-up lease is a means for the lessor to hedge against inflation and future maintenance or operational expenses. For example, a 10-percent rental increase in year five of a ten-year lease.

Sublease: A lease in which the original tenant (lessee) sublets all or part of the leasehold interest to another tenant (known as a subtenant) while still retaining a leasehold interest in the property. Also known as a sandwich lease due to the sandwiching of the original lessee between the lessor and the subtenant. The original lessee is still responsible for the rent if the sublessee defaults.

Tangible Characteristics: Quantifiable, measurable attributes of a property.

Tenant: A person or business that occupies land or property owned by a landlord.

Tenant Improvement Allowance (TIA): The amount a landlord is willing to give to the tenant, typically on a per-square-foot basis, to make improvements to the premises.

Tenant Improvements: The improvements made to a leased space prior to or during a tenant's occupancy, which may be paid for by the landlord, the tenant, or both. These may include adding or removing walls, fixtures, doors, and so forth.

Tenant-Paid Tenant Improvements (TPTI): The cost of improvements paid for by the tenant netted against the landlord's contribution.

Triple Net Lease: A lease agreement where the tenant pays taxes, insurance, and maintenance in addition to rent.

Turnkey: Term referring to the condition of the space being rented that means the space is ready to move into.

Usable Square Feet: The square footage that is directly usable by the tenant including tenant-only restrooms, closets, storage, and other areas used exclusively by the tenant.

Variable Expenses: Costs that change depending on a building's occupancy rate (i.e., utilities).

Zoning: The designation of specific areas by a local planning authority within a given jurisdiction for the purpose of legally defining land use or land use categories. This designation will determine whether a property is commercial, residential, or industrial and can be very specific as to the property's use.

ABOUT THE AUTHOR

TYLER CAUBLE is a commercial real estate broker with a focus on leasing and sales in Nashville, TN. He specializes in applying his expertise and market knowledge to broker retail, office, and industrial properties. Tyler has assisted clients in leasing and purchasing commercial space in all markets of Middle Tennessee and has negotiated on behalf of clients ranging from local businesses with a single location to corporate franchises with hundreds of stores nationwide. Through his writing and speaking engagements, Tyler educates small-business owners and entrepreneurs navigating the world of commercial real estate. For more information, visit: https://tylercauble.com/.

Made in USA - Kendallville, IN
1085113_9781619617230
04.22.2020 0711